PRE-WAR 1619–1819

Seeds of War Sown Early!

I have been uproot[…]
Africa. After a horribl[…]
hold of a ship, here I am on[…]
land, at the hands of a white[…]
I am their slave, that they can b[…]
good can come from such[…]
August 1619, Jamest[…], VA

We declare slavery illegal.
—Rhode Island, 1652

Slaves are hereby declared "real estate."
—State of Virginia, 1705

I is the Infant, from the arms
Of its fond mother torn,
And at a public auction sold
With horses, cows, and corn.

Z is a Zealous man, sincere,
Faithful, and just, and true;
An earnest pleader for the slave—
Will you not be so too?

I have frequently seen [slaves] whipt to that degree that large pieces of their skin have been hanging down their backs, yet I never observed one of them to shed a tear.—**John Brickell**

For months and months at a time we weren't allowed off the farm. Sometimes we would get as far as the gate and peep over. We were told that if we got outside the Padirollers would get us.—**Uriah Bennett**, slave

I haven't anything to say against slavery. My old folks put my clothes on me…they gave me shoes and stockings and put them on me when I was a little boy. I loved them, and I can't go against them in anything. There were things I did not like about slavery on some plantations, whuppin' and sellin' parents and children from each other, but I haven't much to say. I was treated good.
—**Samuel Riddick**

Slaves bring the judgment of Heaven on a country.—**George Mason**

I's just follow the finger. The white man point his finger and I follow it and do.—**Cuffee**, slave

In 1776 Thomas Jefferson signed the Declaration of Independence, which states "all men are created equal." Jefferson was a slave owner.

SOLD!

I didn't come to America to get along with other people from all over and from other states. What do I care about them? I came for opportunity for me and my family. I'm all for fast progress, and bigger cities, and more work. What do I have in common with those hick farmers in the South—nothing. To the Devil with them!—**blacksmith**, Rhode Island

I was an early victim of slave trading. I was born in Benin, in what is now Nigeria, in 1745. At age 11, I was kidnapped from my family and sold into slavery. Later I was sold again to traders and chained on a slave ship bound for America. I was sold to a Virginia planter, and then to a British naval officer, and finally to a Philadelphia merchant who gave me the chance to buy my freedom. As a ship's steward, I traveled widely. I also worked to bring an end to the slave trade. In 1791, I wrote my autobiography.—**Gustavus Vassa**

Laws, I gots to be up at dawn's crack with the baby to head to the fields. That sun sho is hot. Massa says we gots to pick fast today. Cotton is back-breakin' work. It's just one row after another. Gots to stop to nurse the baby as I can, but so the 'seer can't see me.—**Lizzie**, 17, plantation slave

Eli Whitney invents the cotton gin, 1793.

Eli Whitney's invention of the cotton gin made it possible for farmers to make more money and harvest more cotton each year. But it also meant farmers needed more workers. So, they bought slaves from Africa to tend their fields. The cotton gin revolutionized farming…and slavery.

1619…1st slaves to America land in Virginia…1652…Rhode Island declares slavery illegal…1688…1st public protest of slave trade in Pennsylvania…1700

1829…A free black, David Walker, publishes an essay which encourages slaves to revolt. As a result, most southern states make it illegal to teach slaves to read and write…1830…Anti-Slavery Movement begins…1831…Maria Stewart is the first

The Fugitive Slave Act of 1793 demands the return of runaway slaves.

1820–1860 Antebellum=“Before the War”

I don’t know why some people can’t understand the unity of the South. We have our own identity and traditions. Cotton is my crop and I need my slaves to make a successful living. If those darn Yankees came down here they’d see it’s a lot of hot, hard hand-labor, no machine to magically get our crop in and meet the worldwide demand for cotton. Cotton is King, after all!—**plantation owner**, South Carolina

abolitionist: person who worked to do away with slavery

Slavery is a covenant with death and an agreement with hell.—abolitionist **William Lloyd Garrison**, *The Liberator,* Boston

COTTON IS KING!

Some people say “The South was built on the backs of blacks.”

Antislavery newspapers began in 1821 with white editor Benjamin Lundy’s *Genius of Universal Emancipation*. It had six subscribers.

It’s like this: they’s good massas and bad massas. Most white folks not slaves, but be about as po’ as we slaves are! My plantation family’s good to me.—**slave cook**, Louisiana

Reveille is a bugle call that was used to wake up sleeping soldiers at sunrise. During the Civil War, the call was sounded between 4:45-6:00 in the morning! When the last note played, the flag was raised, a gunshot was fired, and the soldiers had to be dressed and ready for roll call.

Slavery was sometimes called a “necessary evil” or the “peculiar institution.”

A plot that involved 9,000 blacks, led by free black Denmark Vesey, was exposed in Charleston, South Carolina in 1822. Vesey and 36 others were executed.

I can’t believe a man like that can be President of these United States! Andrew Jackson is nothing but a common man. Newspapers call him a “barbarian,” “half-wit,” and “tyrant,” and I must say, I agree with them. The people got what they wanted, I guess…a low-class man running this whole nation!—**U.S. citizen**, 1828

Only one of every 20 Northerners was an active abolitionist.

I didn’t have to be told that if a slave struck his master it meant death. Freeborn in North Carolina, but the son of a slave father, I knew slavery firsthand. My hatred of slavery drove me to Boston, where I sold old clothes and subscriptions to the *Freedom’s Journal*. I burned to deliver my own message and in 1829 published my pamphlet, *Walker’s Appeal*.—**David Walker**

In 1831, slave Nat Turner led 70 blacks in a revolt that slaughtered 57 men, women, and children in rural Southampton County, Virginia. Troops rushed in to put down the uprising and killed over one hundred blacks—the innocent as well as the insurrectionists—in a savage massacre. Wild rumors and alarms swept through the South—could this happen again?!—**newspaperman**, North Carolina

I didn’t know I was a slave until I found out I couldn’t do the things I wanted.—Edmund, Georgia

…Virginia declares slaves are “property”…New York puts runaway slaves to death…1725 …Virginia grants slaves right to form own church…1739…Slave

black woman to lecture against slavery…William Lloyd Garrison publishes the first edition of the newspaper, Liberator, which called for emancipation of slaves…Nat Turner leads a slave rebellion in Southampton, Virginia…1833…The American and

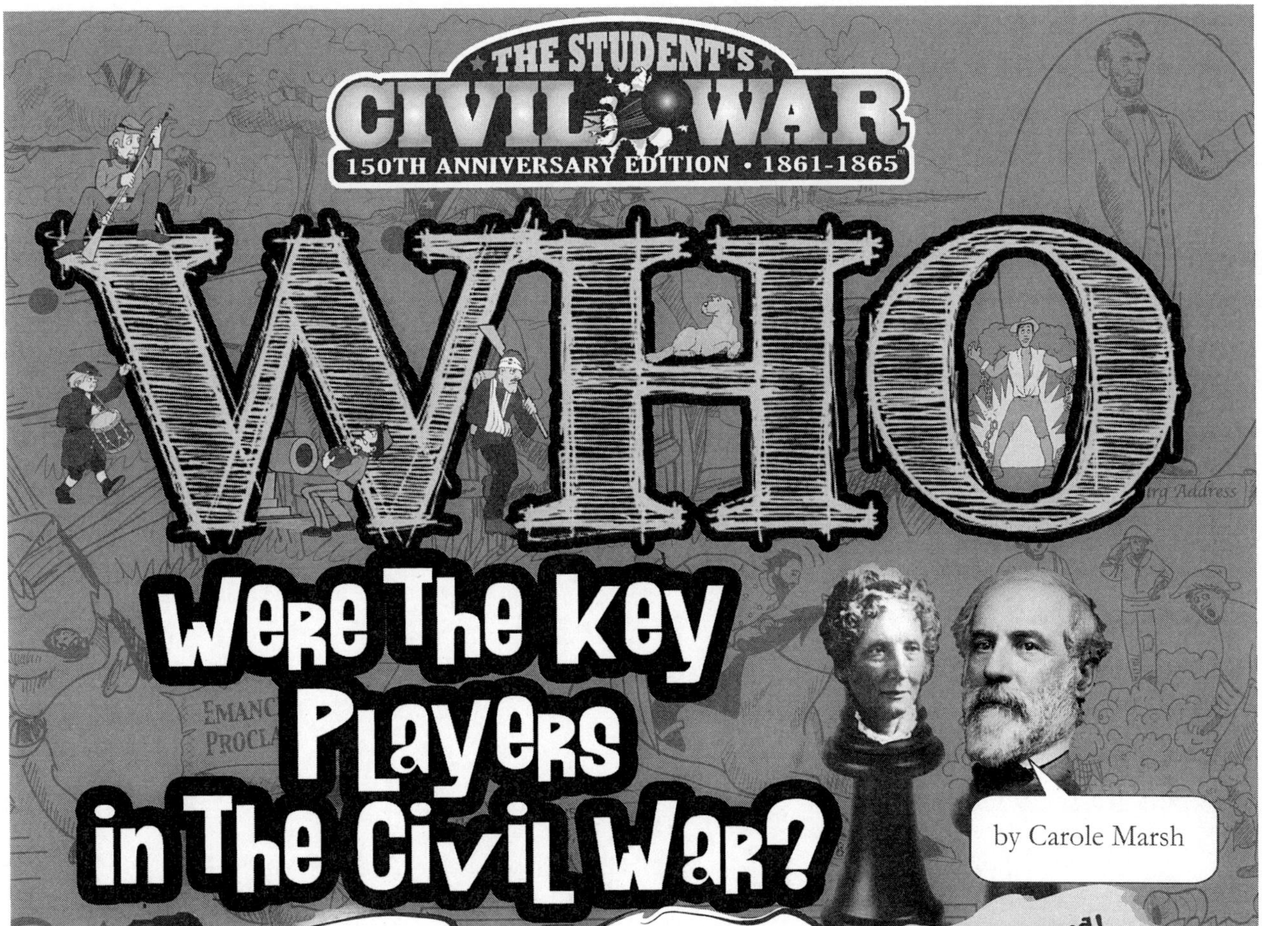

WHO Were The Key Players in The Civil War?

by Carole Marsh

Southerners were polite in calling slavery a "necessary evil." I call slavery a "positive good." I stand by what I said in Congress—slavery is good for blacks!—**John C. Calhoun**, South Carolina senator, 1837

Boo! Boo!

I was born a slave. I worked long and hard for my master 22 years. I finally ran away, and been hiding in a small space in my grandmother's attic for seven years. I'm trying to get to the North and gain my freedom. I finally have my chance. A boat is going to take me there tonight. Perhaps by morning, I'll be free!—**Harriet Jacobs**, North Carolina

How Come?

When I was born I was black.
When I grew up I was black.
When I'm sick I'm black.
When I go out into the sun I'm black.
When I die I'll be black.

But you:
When you were born you were pink.
When you grow up you are white.
When you get sick you are green.
When you go out in the sun you are red.
When you go out in the cold you are blue.
When you die you turn purple.
And you call me colored?

$50 Reward!

Ranaway from the Subscriber, living in the county of Edgecombe, NC, about eight miles north of Tarborough, on the 24th of August last, a negro fellow named Washington, about 24 years of age, 5 feet and 8 or 10 inches high, dark complexion, stout built, and an excellent field hand, no particular marks about him recollected.

sesquicentennial: (noun) [ses-kwi-sen-ten-ee-uhl] a 150th anniversary or its celebration

Maybe he's on the railroad?

Runaways Held in the New Bern, NC, Jail

Two New Negro Men, the one named Joe, about 45 years of age...much wrinkled in the face, and speaks bad English. The other is a young fellow...speaks better English than Joe, whom he says is his father, has a large scar on the fleshy part of his left arm.... They have nothing with them but an old Negro cloth jacket and an old blue sailor's jacket without sleeves. Also...a Negro named Jack, about 23 years of age...of a thin visage, blear-eyed...has six rings of his country marks around his neck, his ears are full of holes.

I was born on a plantation near Fayetteville, North Carolina, and I belonged to J.B. Smith. He owned about 30 slaves. When a slave was no good, he was put on the auction block in Fayetteville and sold.
—**Sarah Louise Augustus**

What man can make, man can unmake.—**Frederick Douglass**, abolitionist

rebellion in South Carolina; 44 slaves killed...1777...Vermont outlaws slavery...1783...Massachusetts outlaws slavery...1792...Kentucky joins Union as slave

the Female Anti-Slavery Societies are formed in Philadelphia...1833...Oberlin College is the first coed college founded to educate African Americans...1837...The first Anti-Slavery Convention of American Women is held in New

It takes an army to do a book. Here's ours:

HEADQUARTERS
Gen. Michele Yother, Gen. Mike Longmeyer, Master Sergeant Cowboy Pilot Bob Longmeyer
Indispensible Right Hand (Wo)man: Nancy "You Gotta Have" Hart *All you really need is heart, you know.* *I know.*

CIVIL WAR CENTRAL
Chief Wrangler: Paige Muh
Sergeant at Art Arms: John Hanson *John's relative walked home from the Civil War.* *Oh, I thought he drove a Volkswagon.*
Scribes, First Class: Whitney Akin, Janice Baker, Sherri Smith Brown
(Battle) Field Artists: Vicki DeJoy, Corie Ferguson, Yvonne Ford, Randolyn Friedlander, Jessica Talley
Erstwhile Intern: Emily Kimbell

That's the important people, right? *Absolutely.*

GENERAL & ACCOUNTING
Muster Masters: Marcie Comeau, Cindy Green, Bri Roden

War bonds, right? *Sure, wanna buy some?* *Yeah, my old Confederate currency ok?*

SALES
Melessa Hill, Pam Morris, Gina Vranesevich, Lori White, Valerie Curry, Jennifer Johnson
Hallelujah Chorus: Denise Morris

MARKETING MILITIA
Head of the One-Million-Man E-mail March: Camille Chasteen
Linda Metoyer, Mark Dean, Tammy Weeks, Jennifer Kelly, Justin Badger

PRODUCTION & FULFILLMENT
Colonel James Barnard *I need fulfilling.* *You always do.*
Dave Guerrero, Pernell Arnold, Kathy Morgan, Jeff Jerabeck

SPECIAL UNIT
Hair and Makeup: Christina Yother *I could use a makeover.* *Ya think?*
Dance and Funny Faces: Grant Yother *My kinda guy!*
Cheerleader: Avery Longmeyer *Cute legs!*
PT, Boot Camp, and Gymnastics: Ella Longmeyer *Whata sweetheart!*
Best Boy: Evan "Da? Da?!" Longmeyer *I thought he was the key grip.* *That, too.*

Private First Class: CAROLE MARSH *Shouldn't she go up at the top?* *It's safer down here…out of the line of fire.* *I'm just sayin…*

In 1849, there were 15 Northern and 15 Southern states. There were more people in the North, but since each state had 2 senators, there was a "stalemate" in the Senate at that time for any effort to pass laws.

I remember all the bricklayers; they all was colored… The men that plastered the City Hall outside and put those columns up in the front…they was slaves, mos' all the fine work…was done by slaves. They called 'em artisans. None of 'em could read, but give 'em any plan an' they could foller it to the las' line.—**John H. Jackson**

Carole Marsh Civil War and Other Sassy Books for Young Readers are available from your favorite school supply or teacher store, almost all of America's fine museum and park stores, at lovely bookstores everywhere, or if all else fails, direct from www.gallopade.com, or call 1-800-536-2GET (that's 2438), extension 11, Miss Cindy.

For further information, trade terms, rights sales, good recipes, advice, and more, please contact:
GALLOPADE INTERNATIONAL
6000 Shakerag Hill
Suite 314
Peachtree City, Georgia
30269

You mean like when the wife stood on the hill and waved her hankie welcoming her Johnny home from the war? *The very same!*
That's in the South, right? *Yes.* *They made up that town name, right?* *Probably.*

I had to try to put an end to this political battle! When the territory of California applied to join the Union in 1849—as a free state—the U.S. had half free and half slave states. To stop this madness, I introduced a bill that would let California be a free state. However, my Compromise of 1850 also said that any new state could choose to be free or slave based on "popular sovereignty" or what the people wanted. After all, a state should have the right to decide what it wants to be, right? My bill passed, but alas, it was only a temporary solution.—Senator **Henry Clay**, Kentucky

See our bibliography and more at www.studentscivilwar.com

state…1793…The Fugitive Slave Act forces return of runaway slaves…Eli Whitney invents the cotton gin…1796…Tennessee joins Union as slave state…1800

York…1839…Joseph Cinque leads a successful revolt on the slave ship, Amistad…1850…Congress passes the Fugitive Slave Act requiring captured runaway slaves to be returned to their owners. Whites now hunt slaves for profit…

A Word from the Author

There's a song that goes *"War! What's it all about? Absolutely nothing!"*

However war is usually about *something*. As you know, the Revolutionary War was all about America wrenching herself away from the final grasp of her mother country of England. It was a war to secure freedom, a new nation, and a new way of life. Later, no one looked back and said, "Hey, maybe we shouldn't have fought that war."

Close to a hundred years after America's founding, people were restless. America was now about a lot of ways of life, many quite different from the others. You might be a plantation owner using slave labor to grow your cotton crop. You might be a mountain woman still living in the wilds of Appalachia. You could be a president trying to run the still new, young, ambitious, and sometimes, even cantankerous and disagreeable country.

Two of the major disagreements of the mid-1800s were slavery and states' rights versus federal rights. Some folks said that they could not survive without slave labor, that they were good to their slaves, and that slavery was now a necessary and permanent part of American life. Others said slavery was wrong and that there was no reason any human being should be owned by another. After all, wasn't America about freedom for all people?

Some Americans thought that states should be able to make their own decisions without so much interference from the federal government in Washington. (Sound familiar?) Other Americans insisted that's what Washington and the federal government were for: to keep all states fair and equal and to solve disputes.

You could say that lanky, teenage America had major growing pains! But America was no longer a "kid." America was at a serious crossroads. Would Americans fight their fellow Americans over these issues? Could such disagreements be resolved by talking, cooperation, compromise, and change? Or would we go to war?

What a curious turn of events—to believe you had to fight your fellow countrymen to the death! Wasn't there any other way? As we know today, getting along and solving problems is much better than going to war. Sometimes, if you are under attack, you may feel you have no choice but to go to war to defend your nation, or to defend others.

Let's just say it was complicated. By the spring of 1861, Americans were actually talking about going to war. They made it sound necessary, even exciting. Many believed it would be a quick war—with their side winning, naturally!

Of course, it didn't happen that way. It was a long war—four years—with terrible tragedies. Slavery was ended. But not before most people "took sides" and fought face-to-face, often against people they knew or were related to, until no one any longer felt that war was a good thing, not even a so-called "necessary" war.

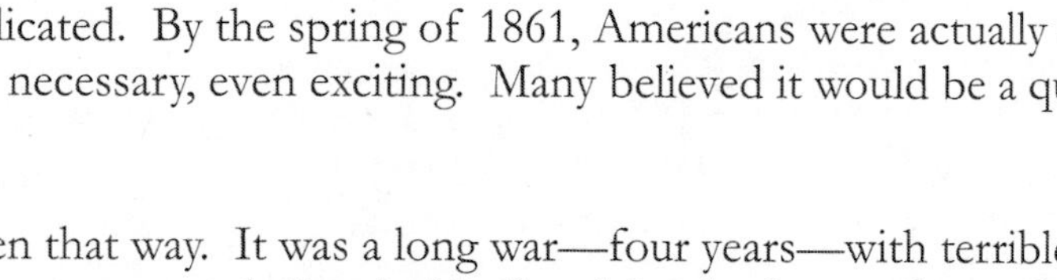

...Free blacks petition Congress to end slavery...Armed slaves rebel in Virginia; most are executed...1803...Ohio joins Union as free state...U.S. buys Louisiana

1853...Sarah Parker Remond is refused a seat in the Howard Athenaeum in New York. She takes the case to the police court, and the defendants are fined...1854...Frances Ellen Watkins Harper delivers her first anti-slavery lecture and publishes

But the person to best tell about America's Civil War is the person who was actually there. You will meet and hear many of those people in this book. Some are real and famous in our history books. Others are "made up" examples of people who found themselves in the midst of war, whether they wanted it or not.

As you read, imagine you are each person. How do you feel? What do you think? And as their stories continue, and you meet some of them again, see how they have changed, how they feel then, and what you think now.

What was the American Civil War about? What did it mean? Was there another way? Was it fun, exciting? Was it fair? Who won? Who lost? What would you have done? What do you think?

Why does it matter what *you* think? Because in the absence of diplomacy, cooperation, collaboration, compromise, understanding, honor, and integrity, it is war, not peace, that always looms on our horizon. The past was in their hands. The future is in yours.

Carole Marsh

Shakerag Hill
Peachtree City, Georgia

Reader,

Entries in *italics* are the actual words of the person.
Entries in regular type have been written based on research of what someone might have said or thought.
Names in **bold** type are actual people.

I've heard rumors of war going around lately. People whispering about soldiers, weapons, strategies. Some even say I've sparked their interest. They want to fight the South and end all the slavery right now. It's the book, I guess. When I wrote Uncle Tom's Cabin, I didn't expect it to be so controversial. I just knew the story needed to be told. I wanted people to know what life was really like for slaves, with good owners and bad owners from Southern and Northern towns. I think I really got people thinking. Most have never heard slavery described like this before.—**Harriet Beecher Stowe**

I am **Tom**, a fictional character from Ms. Stowe's famous book about how slaves were mistreated. In her story, I was murdered in cold blood by plantation overseer Simon Legree. Did such things happen in real life? Were they common or rare? What do you think?

I'm **Franklin Pierce**, elected president in 1852, but not strong enough to lead our nation through the gathering storm of war!

Nine months I was trying to get away.—**Solomon Northup**, slave, born free in New York, kidnapped in 1841 and enslaved on a cotton plantation near Red River in Louisiana.

I find it so hard to believe that Americans might fight Americans! North or South, we are all countrymen, neighbors, brothers, sisters, friends—how can war be? And yet I feel this volcanic groundswell growing beneath the very soil of the land. Will all these eternal arguments over slavery, state versus federal rights, and more just grow louder until we are not talking, but fighting?—**new mother**, Georgia

This footer is a Civil War timeline on top and an African American timeline on the bottom.

NEXT...

My Kansas-Nebraska Act lets new states choose to be free or slave.—**Stephen Douglas**

That fool Douglas did away with the strongest barrier to the expansion of slavery in America!—**Free-Soiler**

I live in "Bleeding Kansas" where we have bloodshed every day over this free/slave issue.

I blame the South for every evil in our nation!—Senator **Charles Sumner**, Massachusetts

*I'll beat you with my cane for what you said!**—**Preston Brooks**, Congressman, South Carolina

*And he did!

Take up your post, Marines! Prepare to storm the arsenal!—**Robert E. Lee**

John Brown, a failure at business and farming, believed the only way to end slavery was through bloodshed. He took over the federal arsenal at Harpers Ferry, Virginia to get slaves to rebel and killed four people in cold blood!—**eyewitness**

Brown wounded and taken prisoner!—**U.S. Marine**

BROWN IS A HERO!—**Northern abolitionists**

BROWN IS A MURDERER!—**Southerners fearful of more such attacks**

We should prepare to fight and defend ourselves! —**community leaders across the South**

John Brown's body lies a-mould'ring in the grave... but his soul goes marching on

John Brown is condemned to death for the crimes of murder and treason; his punishment: to be hanged!—**Virginia court**

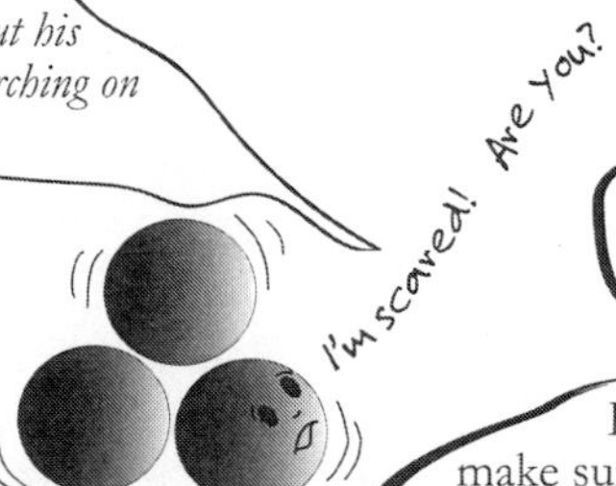

Those crazy Republicans nominated a lanky, backwoods Illinois lawyer named Abraham Lincoln for president!—**Democrat**

He won't be my president, I'll make sure of that.—**Southern slavery supporter**

South Carolina Secedes from the Union/No Longer an American State! December 20, 1860*

*Virginia, Arkansas, North Carolina, Tennessee soon secede

Any state that leaves the Union has broken national law.—**Abraham Lincoln**

joins Union as free state...1817...Mississippi joins Union as slave state...1818...Illinois joins Union as free state...1819...Alabama joins Union as slave state...

War begins...Charlotte Forten Grimke becomes a volunteer teacher of freed men on St. Helena Island in South Carolina...1863...Harriet Tubman leads a military raid on the Combahee River in South Carolina and helps hundreds of slaves escape

President Lincoln's asked me to recruit as many soldiers for the Union army as I can.—**Frederick Douglass**, publisher, *North Star*

The states that left the Union met in Montgomery, Alabama, and organized our own government—the Confederate States of America. Jefferson Davis is our president, and Alexander Stephens, our vice president.—**delegate**, 1861

C.S.A.

We told the federal government they must abandon their forts and arsenals located inside our new Confederate States!—**Owen R.**, SC

We will NOT deal with these so-called Confederate States of America rebellious renegades!—**federal employee**

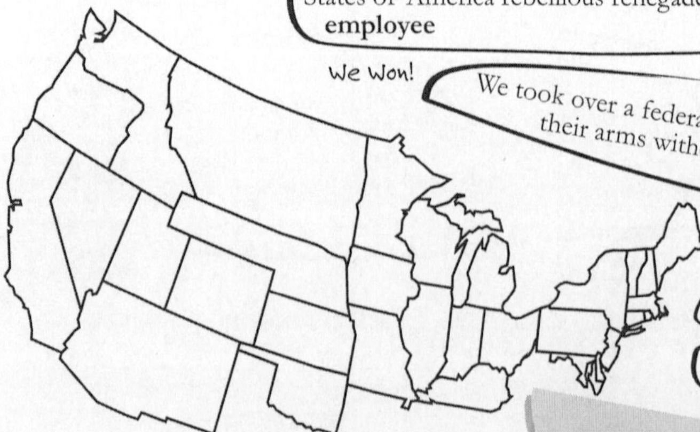

GO!

We took over a federal garrison today! They laid down their arms without a fight!—**Southern militiaman**

We seized a U.S. post today. Can it really be this easy?—**Confederate home guard**

All we ask is to be let alone.—**Jefferson Davis**

Six More States Leave the Union, Join the Confederacy*

*Mississippi, Florida, Alabama, Georgia, Louisiana, and Texas

We will stay in the Union. We are Unionists! Besides, there are Federal troops in our borders.—**Maryland and Missouri citizens**

We declare our state neutral in this war!—**Kentucky governor**

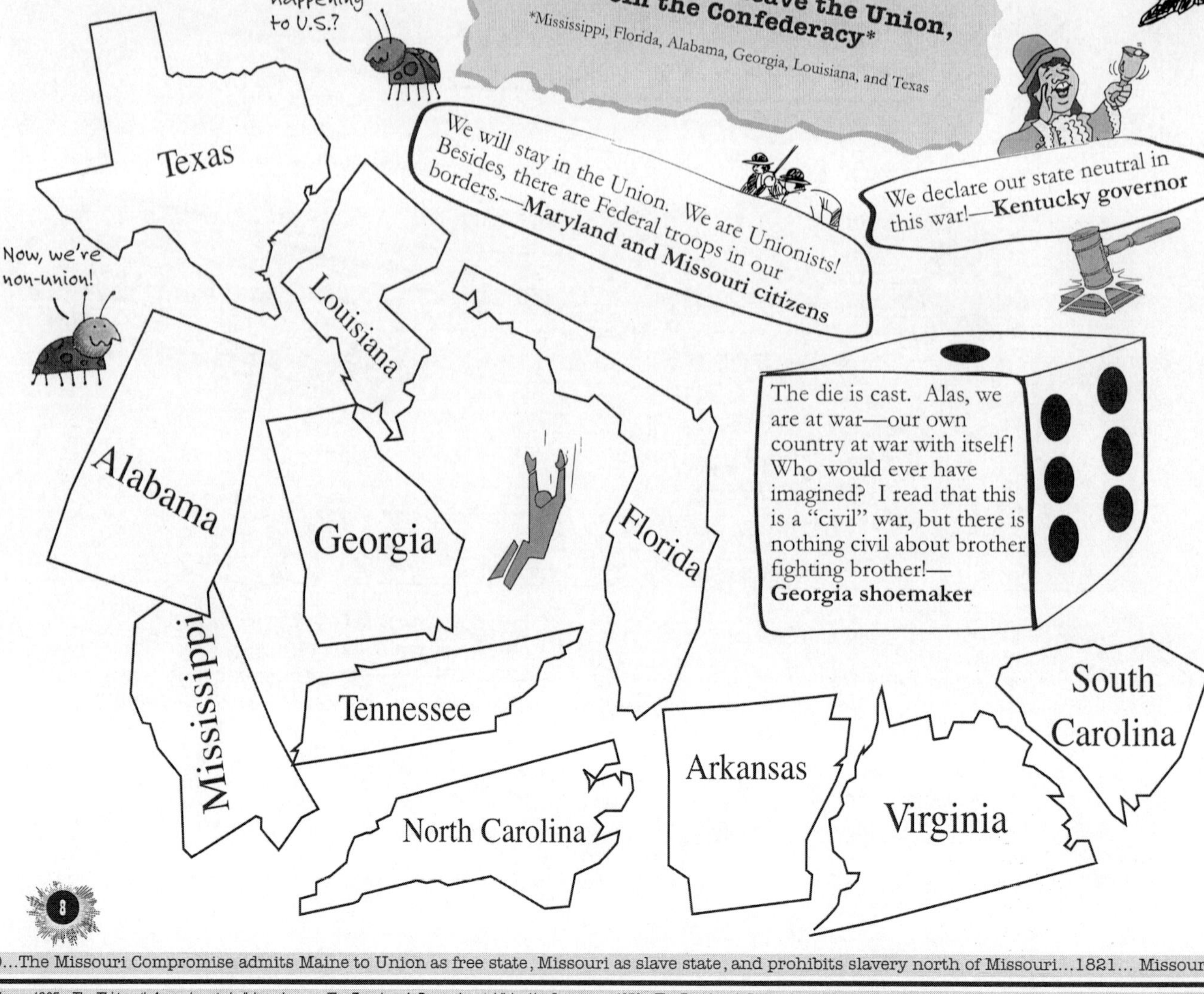

The die is cast. Alas, we are at war—our own country at war with itself! Who would ever have imagined? I read that this is a "civil" war, but there is nothing civil about brother fighting brother!—**Georgia shoemaker**

1820...The Missouri Compromise admits Maine to Union as free state, Missouri as slave state, and prohibits slavery north of Missouri...1821... Missouri

to freedom...1865...The Thirteenth Amendment abolishes slavery...The Freedmen's Bureau is established by Congress...1872...The Freedmen's Bureau is abolished by Congress...1877...The Hayes Compromise ends Reconstruction by

1861

We refuse to surrender Fort Sumter!—**federal troops**, Charleston, South Carolina

We have mounted cannon on the beaches on three sides of Fort Sumter. When the commander still refused to surrender, we launched a 36-hour bombardment!—**Confederate soldiers**

WAR BEGINS!

This is clearly an act of

war!

—Unionists

Sign me up!

We need 75,000 volunteers to counter these Southern rebels!—**Lincoln aide**

This just in!

Victory for the Confederates at Fort Sumter!

Outstanding leadership and war strategies bring Yankees to their knees easily and quickly. Louisiana's own Gen. P.G.T. Beauregard earns our state fame. Spectators praise his commanding skills. They've pinned him "The Little Napoleon" and "The Little Creole" for his unparalleled efforts on the battlefield. Let's hear three Hip-Hip-Hoorays for Gen. Beauregard!—**Louisiana newspaper, 1861**

I am so confused. Do we really have to choose between respect for our Union or invading the very states in which our fellow Americans have lived together in peace as neighbors …until now?—**Virginian**

Uh, oh!

I've received word that the first shots were fired by the Confederate army on Fort Sumter in South Carolina. Some claim I drove the Confederacy to take the first shot. But I cannot claim responsibility for their actions. A war, which I have dreaded for so long, has officially begun.——**Abraham Lincoln**

CIVIL WAR... WE'RE GOING TO WAR!

—Newspaper headline, 1861

Go Rebs!

There ain't been food or supplies and half of Fort Sumter was burnin' from artillery fire. Major Anderson surrendered the fort last night. He told us to bring the Stars and Stripes down and raise a bed sheet instead. We've been ordered to evacuate today, but first we've gotta conduct a 100 gun salute to the American flag. I'm gonna man my cannon, fire, and get off this pile of rocks!*— **Private Daniel Hough**

* *During the official surrender ceremony's 100-gun salute, Private Hough's cannon prematurely discharged and killed him. His was the first death of the Civil War.*

I's **Bessie**. I in't studyin' no wa'. It be quiet here in my Gullah island in Carolina; don't need no mens spillin' no blood 'round here. I got washin' to do, babies to tend, so don't go on 'bout no wa' 'round here.

I don't agree with secession, nor slavery. Just one month ago I was Field Commander for the Union Army. Today, Virginia has seceded from the Union. Therefore, I have to resign all ties to the Union and devote myself to the cause of the South. I am a Virginian and I cannot bring myself to fight against my state, my brothers, my friends, or my family! —**Robert E. Lee**

I worked night and day for 12 years to prevent war, but could not. The North was mad and blind, would not let us govern ourselves, and so the war came.——**Jefferson Davis**

1ST

UNITED WE STAND! DIVIDED WE FALL!

The order has been sent today for troops to gather on the field for battle under my command. Though I'd rather the Union stay together, there seems to be no other solution but war.—**Thomas "Stonewall" Jackson**

The government asks any men with military experience to step up! I volunteered to help my home state, Illinois. They assigned me to recruit men, then quickly promoted me to colonel of an unruly group of Illinois volunteer soldiers. Before I could even fight against a real enemy, I was promoted to brigadier general in the Union Army. It's a real job and a real honor.—**Ulysses S. Grant**

This very day a letter is in the mail for my promotion to captain in the Union Army. I must decline! The great state of Virginia has seceded from the Union. I must fight for *my* state. Therefore I decline the position of captain for the Union and accept the promotion as colonel for the Confederacy.—**J.E.B. Stuart**

War, war, war, that's all these men talk about! I've cried my eyes out for my man, but you know, it's not really fair—why can't I go to war? I don't want to be the one to stay behind and fret, wash, iron, cook, and wait, wait, wait. It's not fair!—**Alice**, 18, Mississippi

I can't wait to go to war! God is on our side, I'm sure. We're right and they're wrong; it's plain as day. This is going to be a nice, little, quick war with a lot of glory for us soldiers.—**Jay**, 19, Ohio

America ready for war? Ha! We have few soldiers and most of those fought back in the War of 1812! Our 140 forts and outposts are spread out over three million square miles. Why we can't even control the Indians out West. Plus we don't really have a real War Department, no accurate maps, and we are so disorganized. Our capitol building doesn't even have a dome!—**Washington bureaucrat**, spring 1861

Why, our nation's capital could be knocked out with a bottle of whiskey!—**Gen. Winfield Scott**

I can't wait to go to war! God is on our side, everyone says! We'll knock those Yanks down in no time and the war will be over and we'll be the heroes…mark my words.—**James** (brother of Jay), 22, North Carolina

I may be 75-years-old and too fat to get on a horse, but I've been a soldier in every conflict since the war of 1812 and I know the best strategies to win. I advised President Lincoln he had to train Union armies to blockade Confederate ports—in the Atlantic and the Gulf and we've got to control the Mississippi River. These blockades will keep goods and supplies out of the Confederacy and cause hardship for their armies and citizens. Cut off food and supplies to kill the Confederacy—an economic stranglehold, just like an anaconda strangles its prey!—**General Winfield Scott**

…I was helping a neighbor sack grain and we heard there was going to be a war meeting at our little log school house…my father was there and objected to my going, so they scratched my name out, which humiliated me…I could rake, and bind and keep up with the men so why couldn't I fight like one too?—**Elisha Stockwell**, 15

The Confederacy ready for war? You must be kidding? First we have to build an army and out of what? We are not really a "country" but a bunch of states with militia and home guards. Also, we just moved the capital from Montgomery, Alabama to Richmond, Virginia—only 100 miles from Washington! —**Alabama physician**

My master and I traveled all the way from California just to join the Confederate Army. Our first night in the camp, I followed my master into his tent and snuggled up close to him. All the soldiers laughed at me and I noticed the man I had followed wasn't my master. It was the commander! Hee—Haw!—**Jason the Donkey**

Most of these soldiers look at me like I'm crazy. A woman planning military strategies? Give them ten minutes with me, though, and they see why President Lincoln requested my assistance! I know politics, and war. I've been mapping out a plan for the Union to invade the Confederacy. Lincoln thought a push down the Mississippi River might be wise. But I see it a different way: push the Confederate troops back along the Tennessee River. I hope Lincoln values this plan, because it's the only way the Union will successfully win this war.—**Anna Ella Carroll***

** Anna's war strategy was sent to Lincoln in 1861. Four years later, Ulysses S. Grant used the exact strategy to push Confederate troops to surrender at Appomattox Court House, VA. Anna never received credit for creating the strategy.*

There are plenty of men spies, and there are even some women spies. But I'll bet that I am the only spy that is a dog! My human, Mrs. M. and I went on a walk to go see Gen. Beauregard. On our way, Confederates stopped and searched us to make sure we didn't have any secret documents. They had no idea that I had a secret report hidden beneath a fake layer of fur that Mrs. M. had sewn onto my back!—**Dog Spy**

My uniform doesn't fit. Pants too long! Flannel shirt too short and itches like mad. Hat feels like a bag on my head. I'm dog-tired of doin' drills over and over again. I complained but they say I gotta learn to OBEY! Three weeks of this and it's on to Washington. I'll cut down my uniform and go, but I got no patriotism inside.—**Warren Lee Goss**, Union soldier

Have you seen the new sketches in *Harper's* Magazine? They're by a young man, Homer-something. There's a magnificent one of a bucking horse with a Union general staring ahead. I think this young man's got some talent!—***Harper's* Magazine subscriber describing Winslow Homer's illustrations.**

It's like David and Goliath: The North has plants and industry, 22 million citizens, railroad lines. The South has only 9 million folks, many of them slaves, no money —good luck!—**New York businessman**

We gol'darn Southerners are true patriots! Why we fought the Brits and won! We have real military leaders like Lee and Jackson, and we have lots of land—bring on them Yanks!—**Tennessee tobacco planter**

I just didn't listen to my parents' grumblin' when I talked about joinin' the Confederate troops. Finally, I wore 'em down. I was only 16, which Momma said was entirely too young to be goin' to war, but I wanted to fight. I'm a little ashamed to admit it, but the day they dropped me off at the train to report for duty, I hid by myself and cried.—**George Gibbs**, 16

I was part of a regiment that had just won the battle in Lexington, Kentucky. I was so excited—the whole regiment was laughing, bragging, and getting rowdy in the streets! Part of our winning tradition was to drag the Union flag through the streets, just to let everyone know who was boss. But today, something happened that surprised me. A crazy 17-year-old Union girl named **Ella Bishop** ran up to me, grabbed the flag, wrapped herself in it, and yelled that she would rather die than surrender it! I stood in shock as she ran off. I guess she showed us who was boss!—Confederate soldier

When the Yankees set a trap for John Mosby, I set out on foot to warn him. Luckily, I warned Mosby in time and saved his life. I then began to hide messages and money for Mosby underneath a rock near my home. Those Yankees never caught me. They were as dumb as that rock I used as my hiding spot!—**Laura Ratcliffe**

I can't wait to join the Army! Hope the war don't end 'fore I get in!—**North Carolina boy**, 16

After my husband died of an accidental gunshot wound, I decided to join the Confederate army. I disguised myself as a man and joined the battalion of troops known as the "Arkansas Grays." Now I am the lieutenant of the unit and about to lead my troops at Manassas. No one knows that their leader is actually a woman!—**Loreta Janeta Velazquez**

William Lloyd Garrison publishes The Liberator...Slave rebellion in Virginia leads to tougher slave laws...1832...Congress passes new tariff law, benefiting

College of Pennsylvania...1909...The NAACP is founded...1920...The Nineteenth Amendment gives women the right to vote...1935...Federal Writers' Project established by Franklin Roosevelt...fieldworkers were assigned to travel through

Bull Run or Manassas?

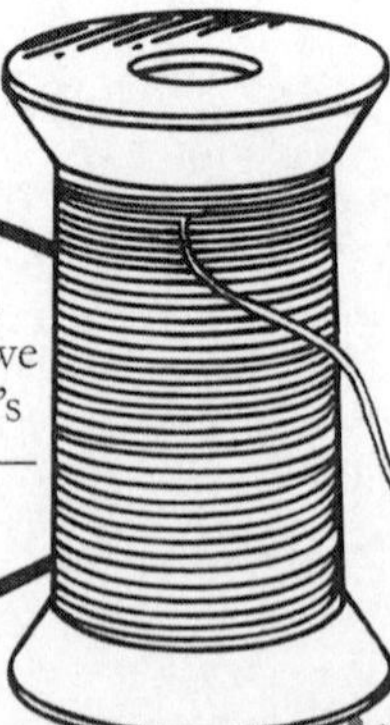

This is crazy! We are not ready to fight but we are fighting. Dressed in a ragtag mess of unmatched uniforms, we sometimes fire on our own fellows. It's just mobs of men, too eager for war! —**South Carolina seamstress**

We're just a group of men with horses. But we're good riders and know this land like the back of our hands. We're going to scout, make surprise attacks, and raid the enemy—whatever works to get the Union off our land! We'll make the Virginia Cavalry infamous, courtesy of our leader, Colonel Stuart.—soldier

I hope God is on our side, but I must have Kentucky!—**Abraham Lincoln**

I'm about to lead a company into battle, something I've never done. My recruits are so green. We're not ready but Lincoln says fight—and it's just a mere 30 miles from our nation's capital!—**Gen. Irwin McDowell**, U.S. Army

What a hot day for a battle! We are charging Henry House Hill. Our sides are pretty even. But what's this?! Confederates are holding that hill like a stone wall! Our side is retreating! Why even the generals, as well as the privates, are scampering, tails-between-their-legs back to Washington—in the North's first defeat!—**Edmond F.**, rifleman

My spies keep me posted on what McDowell is up to! He's headed to Manassas Junction. But I have my troops already set up on the creek called Bull Run*.—Confederate **General Pierre G.T. Beauregard**

*The Union referred to this battle as First Manassas; the Confederates as First Bull Run.

It was the first battle my troops encountered. I commanded them to hold steady and face their enemy without fear and flinching. We held our ground and stared into the faces of the oncoming troops with nothing but bravery and confidence, feigned though it was.—**Thomas "Stonewall" Jackson**

I saw my troops begin to waver. Fear trembled though their bodies as the Union Army marched toward them, guns pointed. I looked over and saw Jackson's men standing calm, dead still. I called out to my men, There stands Jackson like a stone wall. Rally behind, Virginians!—**Colonel Bernard Bee***

* Colonel Bee's remark caught on. Thomas was called "Stonewall" Jackson for the rest of his life.

Oh, Jane, you can't believe! We took a picnic and went to watch the war. I thought it would be fun, entertaining. Quick, easy, and bloodless. And that our side would win. We left as quick as we saw the bloody reality of it all. Later, I heard 868 killed, and more than 2,500 wounded! —Washington wife

President Davis,
I am writing with all due respect. We have gained another victory at Bull Run, the second of many for the Confederates. Although we pushed the Union to retreat, we missed an opportunity to overtake them. My men are exhausted from fighting and have little food and supplies. I am confident that with ample rations, my men would have been more successful in this battle. Perhaps the Confederacy should consider first taking care of their young soldiers?
Sincerely,
Gen. P.G.T. Beauregard

I just kept nursing those men. Wasn't even paying attention to which side was which. When I crossed the line into Confederate Army territory, they opened fire on me. But a few gunshots hitting the ground weren't enough to make me stop. I just tied my handkerchief to a stick and raised it as a truce flag, then kept right on working.—**Mary Jane Safford**

Gen. George McClellan named general-in-chief, Union Armies Believes only he can win war…builds Army of the Potomac…let's wait and see.—soldier

A picnic?!

The sound of soldiers marching in the street below my hotel room woke me up that morning. I had been humming the song "John Brown's Body," the day before, wishing for some new words to the old tune. Suddenly, ideas started flowing into my head, beating in rhythm with the marching soldiers below. In the early morning light I grabbed some paper and a pen and wrote, *Mine eyes have seen the glory of the coming of the Lord*. The words just poured into place. Soon, the lyrics were published in the *Atlantic Monthly* and men were singing my new song all over the North. They called it the "Battle Hymn of the Republic." —**Julia Ward Howe***

*The first verse of the "Battle Hymn of the Republic":
Mine eyes have seen the glory of the coming of the Lord;
He is trampling out the vintage where the grapes of wrath are stored;
He hath loosed the fateful lightning of His terrible swift sword;
His truth is marching on.
Glory! Glory! Hallelujah! Glory! Glory! Hallelujah!
Glory! Glory! Hallelujah! His truth is marching on.

We are fighting at Wilson's Creek, Missouri. We are wearing our blue* uniforms, which confused the Federals, so we beat them! Their captain, Nathaniel Lyon, was killed. Of course, we lost 1,300 men in the skirmish—same as them.—soldier

*Later, gray would become the Confederate uniform color

The entire state of Missouri is now under military control. All slaves of Southern sympathizers are to be freed. Irregular Southern troops known as guerrillas and bushwhackers will be executed if captured.—**Gen. John Charles Frémont**

Oops...

Dear father, Have you heard of the new rifle weapon? I've not seen one yet. We fight with anything we have: shotguns, butcher knives, axes, blunderbusses. After my buddy, Jed, was killed, I got his Springfield musket—it even had a bayonet attached. I hear the new rifle will let us shoot farther and hit harder. In the meantime we are in the trenches pretty much slaughtering each other face-to-face. More soon, your son, Samuel…

We respectfully asked the U.S. Congress to make the 50 western counties of western Virginia a new state of the Union, our state to be called Kanawha* after our river.—delegate

*Approved in 1863, the state's final name was West Virginia

Kana-what?

This rebellion cursed city of Nashville wants me to take my Union flag down from my roof. They said if I did not, they would fire the house to bring it down. "Load me my shotgun!" I told my husband. He did so with 16 buckshot in each barrel. Now, I will take the responsibility of guarding that flag. Whoever attempts to pass my door on their way to the roof for the star-spangled banner, under which my four uncles fell at King's Mountain during the Revolutionary War, must go over my dead body!—**Hetty McEwen**

I am a daughter of the South. Richmond. My family all live there. But I cannot defend slavery. A war for its perpetuation is utterly unjust. All of my sympathies are on the side of the Union and its defenders. I will volunteer to sew or nurse or do whatever I am called on to do to help the Union be victorious! **Elizabeth Mendenhall**, hospital volunteer in Cincinnati

The Nation's war cry: forward to Richmond! The Rebel congress must not be allowed to meet there on the 20th of July. By that date the place must be held by the national army.—**Horace Greeley**, editor, New York Tribune, one of the most influential newspapers in the country

If it must be so, take it freely. I had hoped to live here in peace and quiet, and never to leave this sweet spot, which my husband has taken so much delight in making beautiful. But if my country demands it, take it freely. You have my consent.—**A Union soldier's wife**, on learning that the Army needs to destroy her grounds and gardens to build earthworks and a battery to defend Washington, D.C.

King's Mountain

WAR!

forms Female Anti-Slavery Society…Theodore Weld forms American Anti-Slavery Society…Ohio's Oberlin College 1st to admit blacks…1835… South Carolina

people organize to press their demands for justice… President Roosevelt issues an executive order against discrimination of workers in defense industries and government…1942… Margaret Walker wins the Yale Award for Young Poets for her

I stood in the middle of the street for hours in the hot broiling sun with the other Union prisoners as dozens of citizens jeered us. Suddenly, a boy of about 12 slyly touched my sleeve and asked, *Are you from New England?* I told him I was born in Massachusetts. *So was my mother,* he replied. *She was a New England girl, and she was what you call a school ma'am; she married my father, and I'm their boy; but how she does love New England and the Yankees, and the old United States! And so do I.* I had nothing to give the boy to strengthen his loyalty but a button from my coat, which I cut from my breast and slipped into his hands.—**a Union Major POW**

Oh, that's him! That's him! It's pa! It's pa! He's going! He's going! He's gone!—**A Little Girl**, sobbing as a new regiment of Union volunteers march out of town headed for Washington D.C.

I crossed enemy lines to find you my dearest husband on the wretched battlefield, nearly dead from your grevious wounds. You said, *I knew you would come.* For months now, I have lived with you, tending your wounds, in the bowels of Richmond's Libby Prision. Crowded, dreary, cheerless, bare brick walls and unceiled roof, and dirty floors where sufferers pine and languish – hope and life dying from their breasts. I will stay by your side in this filthy Confederate prision. I will not leave until we can leave the soil of Virginia together.—**Fanny Ricketts** to her husband Union Capt. James B. Ricketts

POW = Prisoner of War

1862

War explodes in fury in Tennessee! Our Gen. Albert Sidney Johnston tries to defend a 300-mile line from Cumberland Gap, Virginia to the Mississippi River with a measley 25,000 troops. We try to defend all points and so can defend no points! We just can't give the Union control of our rivers!—**Confederate officer**

The whole land which was smiling with plenty and peace has since become a vast arena of deadly strife.—**young Virginia captain**

Just look at that U.S. Grant! He's a puny, quiet guy, but I hear a tough commander…we'll see!—**Confederate officer**

Wimp?

I couldn't get out of the water! It pulled me under with such force. All I could think was Cordelia, poor, sweet Cordelia. She'd be all alone. I shouldn't have left her alone. I came to the South to help wounded soldiers but now I'm a wounded man that no one can fix. Poor, sweet Cordelia…—**Lewis Harvey**, Governor of Wisconsin

Seven gunboats and 15,000 soldiers have taken Fort Henry under Grant's direction! Mother Nature helped us with the rising river. It took no time to take down the less than 100 Confederates inside that sinking pile of dirt!—**Union soldier**

I thought farmin' cotton was hard, but I'm plumb wore out and filthy as a warthog from building dirt forts on bluffs of the Tennessee and Cumberland rivers. Fort Henry and Fort Donelson they call them, but we ain't got enough men or guns for 'em.—**Confederate soldier**

When he headed down South I was worried about him, but I never thought his life would end that way. He drowned in the Tennessee River. There were no gunshots or cannons. You wouldn't even know the war was in full force. When I first heard the news, all I could do was cry. But now, I'm ready to follow in his footsteps. He wanted to help sick soldiers, so that's just what I'll do. I've been appointed Sanitary Agent for Wisconsin. I may not be a nurse, but I'll make sure those soldiers are comfortable and happy.—**Cordelia Harvey**

Oh, Lord, Gen. Buckner has raised a flag of truce here at Fort Donelson, just a week after we lost at Fort Henry. He asked Gen. Grant what terms he would offer us. We await the answer.—**Confederate soldier**

My mama said my daddy got killed fighting with the Union army. I was sad cause I'm never gonna see him again. Then she said we had no money and no place to live on our own. After taking money from a man, she left me at the train station and now I am ridin' in this boxcar with a bunch of other children like me headed West to who knows where. They say we're gonna work on a farm to earn money for our keep. I ain't sad no more—I'm just scared.—**orphan**

Unconditional surrender!—Gen. Grant to Gen. Buckner*

*U.S. Grant's nickname became Unconditional Surrender!

If they would just listen to me! We could have won!

More than 13,000 of us Confederate prisoners are being marched off*.—soldier

*Largest number of POWs (Prisoners of War) captured until World War II.

When the Union decided to attack Fort Donelson, my superiors, John Floyd and Gideon Pillow, panicked! Floyd was a politician, Pillow a civilian. Neither one knew much about war. I had general knowledge, but as third in command I had no say. In their panic, they broke out of the fort and joined forces with Johnston to attack Grant's army. To my surprise, their plan actually worked. Well, it would have worked, if Floyd hadn't lost his nerve and retreated back into the fort. He arranged a surrender. How these men earned their positions, I don't know. I suppose I'll take over as commander of the fort now, if we ever gain it back from Union control.—**Simon B. Buckner**

I fought as "Albert" in the Illinois Volunteer Infantry. No one knew I was a woman until I broke my leg at the age of 66. Authorities kept my gender a secret. I was allowed to collect invalid soldier's pension and live at the Soldiers' and Sailors' Home.—**Jennie Hodgers**

I bet I surprised those guys!

Them women were standin' in the middle of those tracks front of that old wood trestle bridge, wavin' their lanterns wildly in the night. I yanked on those brakes, and the trained screeched to a halt jest in time. Those two women said a gang of guerrilla Confederates had infested the neighborhood. Knew the train was comin' loaded with Union soldiers. They'd fired that bridge jest enough to make it weak but still standin'. We would've plunged to our deaths. Those women set out in the dead o' night to warn us. They refused the money the soldiers offered for savin' our lives. They jest wanted a safe passage back home. They got it.—**train Engineer**, carrying the 27th Iowa from Corinth to Jackson, TN

Don't be afraid, Captain, I can drum, he said when his mother asked if he could join our company. And he could. The 12-year old boy we called Little Eddie, whose father had been killed by Rebels and whose mother was destitute, became a favorite with all the men in the company. But after the fight at Wilson's Creek, I heard his drum beat for help in the deep ravine where we had fought. *Don't leave me, Captain.* He began to cry. *I can't walk.* A cannon ball had shot off his feet! The dead Confederate soldier beside him had taken off his buckskin suspenders and corded the little fellow's legs below the knees, then lay down to die beside him. Enemy scouts came upon us and took me prisioner. I asked them to take care of Eddie. They carried him away with great care, but by the time I reached the enemy camp, he was dead.—**Union captain**

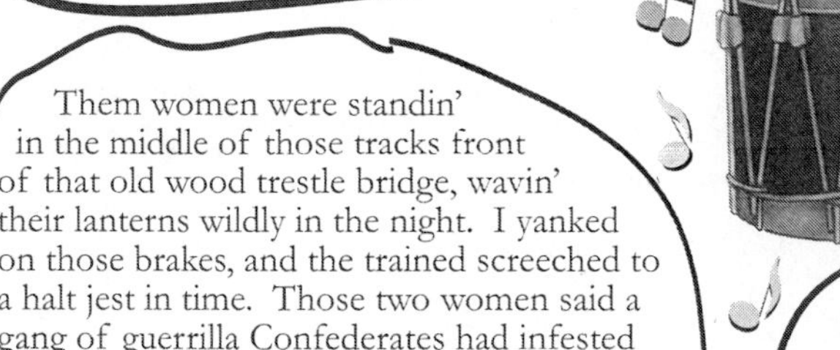

It is April now and spring is peeping out. Gen. Grant has us camping at a place called Shiloh, named for a nearby meetinghouse. We are near the Tennessee-Mississippi border, waiting for Gen. Don Carlos Buell's army, so we can whip some Confederate be-hind over at Corinth. Can't wait!—**Union soldier**

It sure is breezy in this tent!

The tide has turned! Gen. Buell's men have arrived at last! Bloody and dead Rebs hang over tree limbs and lay limp in the ravines.—**Union soldier**

Yow! I can see our surprise attack has stunned the Union troops! Casualties are by the hundreds each hour. Heard a rumor our Gen. Johnston has bled to death from a bullet wound!—**Confederate soldier**

We are surely outnumbered two to one. Our captain told us to abandon the field. We are bloody, weary, or dead. So this is war…—**Confederate soldier**

When my Army of Ohio arrived at Shiloh, we saw a number of Grant's men cowered at the edge of the battlefield. Only then did we realize the gravity of the battle before us. My 23,000 men entered alongside Grant's men. We successfully pushed the Confederates back on the second day. The battle would not have been a success if it had not been for me. Grant was weak and on the verge of defeat. Thanks to my men, the Union has gained another victory.—**Gen. Buell***

*Despite General Buell's confidence, his helpfulness in the Battle of Shiloh is widely debated. Although he did aid Grant, many historians do not give him credit for gaining victory for the Union.

I guess you could say we spent our honeymoon on the battlefield. My husband and I were wed just days before he was called to fight. I decided if he was going, I would too. I help with the troops and do what I can. One morning I was cooking pancakes on the griddle when a cannon ball blasted out from nowhere and blew up the trees behind me. I knew a battle would be coming that day so I cooked all the faster…I needed to make sure my husband had a full belly. Suddenly I heard shouts that the Rebels were attacking. I ran to my husband, stuffed the pancakes in his haversack, and took cover.
—**Belle Reynolds**

Dear mother,
I am doing all right so far
without my left leg. I hear
4,000 men died at Shiloh, and
four times that wounded, like
me, and likely to die, which I
refuse to do unless infection
takes hold. No more soldiers
have ever been killed or wounded
in any America battle. Surely
this is the worst of it? All I
know, is we won't ever give up
now. Of course, maybe the
other side won't either. Hoping
to be home in mostly one piece
soon, your son

Those eleven Confederates came to m' house. When they saw m' husband was a Union volunteer, they started helpin' themselves to everthing in m' home. Ran down the chickens, kilt 'em, ate 'em, and cut up m' carpets for horse blankets. I watched and waited. When they slept, suspectin' nothin' from me, I removed their weapons and stood with two loaded muskets by the door, demandin' their surrender. One springed toward me. He's dead. I've marched them here, Colonel. They're your prisioners of war.—**Union soldier's wife**

This day was a disaster, to say the least. With Johnston wounded, I took command of the Confederate troops. We pushed the Union back throughout the day. Their forces were weakened. I commanded my men to pull back and make camp outside of the battlefield for the night. I calculated that the Union troops would be easily defeated in the morning. Upon waking, however, I heard the battle still raging…Grant's army is stronger than I thought! My men are weary and the battlefield covered with bloody bodies. I decide to order a retreat. We stumble off the battlefield too tired to continue the fight.—**Confederate Gen. P.G.T. Beauregard**

Who does that man think he is? Just because he has "General" before his name, that don't make him nothin'. Our boys fightin' all day. Ten thousand were killed. Ten thousand! And he just lets them retreat. I'll tell you what he did, he just gave the victory over to the Union. The Confederates should have won Shiloh. Who does he think he is?!—**Confederate supporter** on P.G.T. Beauregard's actions at the Battle of Shiloh

Most boys my age are at home pretending to be soldiers. Not me! At nine-years-old I ran away to join the Union army. They told me I was too young and small to fight, but I wouldn't go home. I hid with the baggage on a train carrying soldiers. Soon, I became the drummer for the 22nd Michigan Regiment. I even got paid $13 a month! My first battle was the battle of Shiloh. Bullets flew everywhere! Some men ran away, but not me! I didn't even run when my drum got shattered by a bullet. The troops were so impressed they made me a sergeant and gave me the nickname Johnny Shiloh.—**Johnny Clem**

The Yanks have to send their babies to fight. — **Rebel soldier's** assessment of Johnny Clem

After our defeat at Shiloh, I must keep order among the men. I will not tolerate deserters. In fact, I will not tolerate disobedience of any kind! Yes, the Conscription Act has extended the enlistment period from one year to three years. Yes, the men are upset. But it's the law, and they had better obey it. I don't care if they hate me. I will not hesitate to have them shot. Not for a minute!
—**Gen. Braxton Bragg**

It's raining and we slog through an all-day battle at Williamsburg, slowing our advance more than ever. We trudge through muck and mud. At least we have twice the troops of the Confederates, who are in retreat, but somehow I don't feel good about this.—infantryman

The president is so exasperated! McClellan has spent six months building and training the Army of the Potomac. Yet instead of taking this mighty force into battle, he parades. His battle plan seems to be not to battle at all! He must think this is some kind of chess match, not a war. Finally, Lincoln has demanded that general to fight!—aide

Gen. McClellan sent a hot air balloon up in the sky every day to survey the Confederate army's position. Rebels really enjoyed shooting at the balloon. Later, the Confederacy had a balloon made of donated silk dresses!

I do not understand our general. Instead of marching due south to attack the Confederates, McClellan is taking us to the Virginia coast by boat! More than 450 vessels of all kinds have been loaded with 70,000 troops, 300 cannon, thousands of horses, and tons of supplies.—soldier

What?! The Confederates are not at Manassas as we thought—they are here right in front of us! Standing on the same peninsula! Right in front of our goal—the city of Richmond. Gen. McClellan is shocked!—captain

OOPS

Some call it Seven Pines, some call it Fair Oaks. We are a mere nine miles from Richmond. Gen. Joseph E. Johnston orders us to attack! We have half the soldiers the Federals do, yet we have stopped their advance!—Confederate soldier

I passed the night without fear, though sleep was driven away by the continual tramp of troops passing along the streets and the rumbling of artillery and baggage wagons. This continued, with little cessation, for the next two or three days, until the whole rebel army had passed through town; and as I sat at my window, watching them hour after hour, I could almost imagine that all the beggars in the world had congregated in that mighty host, so ragged were they, so filthy and squalid in appearance. Yet, these men were by no means ruffians. Seeing me at the window, they would sometimes stop, and ask politely for food; and when I gave whatever I had at hand, they received it with gratitude.—**Charlotte McKay**, Union nurse, Virginia

Union commander Ormsby M. Mitchel told us today we are allowed to give ourselves a las' name. We slaves ain't never had no las' names. I'm gonna think long and hard 'bout this.—**freed slave**

I'd been holding his hand as he lay near death in the Washington hospital when I learned his mother was in the room. She'd traveled all the way from Rhode Island to be with him. "He is very weak and probably will not know the difference," I told her, putting her hand in his. But immediately, he opened his eyes and said, *That feels like my mother's hand. Who is this beside me? It is my mother. Turn up the gas (lamp), and let me see my mother!*—**Nurse** to a dying Union soldier

No, doctor, he's not dying; he's coming to life; he will live if we don't give him up. This wound on his head won't amount to anything if we can get him warmed up. Don't you see he's been nearly frozen to death while faint from loss of blood? But he's coming on finely, and by and by, you can take off his arm, and the man may get well. Who knows but he has a mother or a sister to love him, and thank you or me some day for a son or brother saved?—**Nelly Chase**, nurse at Fredericksburg

Jefferson Davis hired me as a maid. He thought that since I was black, I didn't know how to read or write. He sure was wrong! I read all his documents and leaked the information to the Union army.
—**Mary Elizabeth Bowser**

I've decided that Gen. Robert E. Lee is the best man to command the Confederate troops in Virginia. They're our biggest group of men. But these men, some still boys in mismatched uniforms, are ready to fight with only hatchets and shovels. None have military experience. If we're going to win this war, I need someone who can transform this group of mangy men into a real, respectable army.—**Jefferson Davis**

A Confederate captain marched 100 men with loaded guns up to our door and made a formal demand for that broad and beautiful striped bunting that floated over our cottage. It proclaimed that our hearts, and hopes, and fears were with the Union cause and troops. We came to the door, each of us armed with a revolver and holding that glorious banner between us. We'll never surrender our flag to traitors, and we'll shoot the first Rebel that pollutes it with his touch we told the captain. They left.—**Maria and Mattie Taylor** in the much-divided town of Danville, KY

GOOD
BAD

Our General Johnston is wounded! Some general named Robert E. Lee is taking over. President Jeff Davis says so. This better be a good decision!—
Confederate captain

The great Gen. Johnston was badly wounded today at the battle of Fair Oaks. It is a great loss to the Confederate Army. President Davis asked me to take the general's place as commander of the Army of Northern Virginia. It is a group of some of the finest soldiers I've ever known and I intend to lead them to victory!—**Robert E. Lee**

I was a good general before, and after, my wound. I won the first battles of the war at Bull Run, commanding the Army of Virginia. But at the Seven Days Battle I was shot in the chest. Everyone assumed it was fatal. Gen. Lee took my place of command. Somehow, however, I survived the bullet. Now I wonder, what if I hadn't been shot that day. Would I now be commander of the Confederate Army? Would I lead those men to victory time and time again? I can't help but compare myself to the man who replaced me. Gen. Lee is a great general indeed, maybe much better than I could be…—**Gen. Joseph E. Johnston**

I'm not very educated or sophisticated, but I do what I can for my state. I'm a proud spy for the Confederate army. I've only been captured once, and I escaped by stealing a musket and killing the guard.—**Nancy Hart**

I am sent by Gen. Lee to check on the Union troops and have returned with that information, as well as prisoners!
—**Gen. James Ewell Brown "Jeb" Stuart**

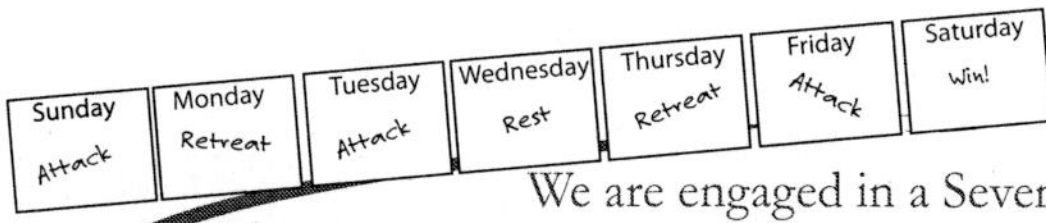

We are engaged in a Seven Day's Campaign, one dogged battle after another. I have Gen. Jackson with me and we are driving hard through Mechanicsville, Gaine's Mill, White Oak Swamp, Frayser's Farm and Malvern Hill. We have only won one battle, suffered 20,000 casualties, but pushed the Army of the Potomac out of the way and saved Richmond!—**Gen. Robert E. Lee**

Luck is with us! The Army of the Potomac has returned to Washington. Generals Lee and Jackson have joined up! Now we'll give Gen. Pope a run for his money!—**Confederate soldier,** Cedar Mountain, near Culpepper, Virginia

I have a mind to relieve Mr. Beauregard from all his responsibilities in the Confederate Army. That Creole's arrogant manner has been more than I can take! He is too confident on the battlefield. His pride is much greater than his skills. Mr. Beauregard is far from a Southern gentleman, and I expect more from a leader in this Confederacy.—**Confederate President Jefferson Davis***

*Although Gen. Beauregard was dismissed from duty, two months later he rejoined the battle. Overall he is considered to be an unsuccessful general.

Because I was a slave, I was not allowed to learn how to read or write. Every morning, I would pretend to go to the fields to work. Instead, I sneaked off to school! I loved to learn new words. When I was 14, the Union army took control of where I lived. My family and hundreds of other slave families climbed aboard ships headed to the North. The captain of the ship asked me if I knew how to read and write. He was surprised when I said yes! I was given the task of teaching the other slaves how to read.—**Susie King Taylor**, Savannah, Georgia

Today I knelt by a young man to heal his wounds and as I looked into his hurting face, a bomb hit him. He blew to pieces before my very eyes! I can't understand why I wasn't hurt…and he lost his life. This war is endlessly cruel and unfair. — **Annie Etheridge**

Old "Stonewall" has us march behind a mountain range, out of sight. What a ploy! Like ghosts or magicians, we reappear behind the Union army and attack! With a CRACK! and a BOOM! and a POWWWWWWW! we destroy the Federal's enormous supply depot at Manassas Junction!—**Confederate soldier**

Yeah, I know Gen. Jackson well. Did you know he was an orphan, not such a good student at West Point but later a professor! Very religious. He excels at pounding attacks, strict secrecy, and great sweeping flank marches—that's how he won. His infantry will march as long and far as horsemen!—**schoolmate**

We have two Stonewall Jacksons in our army. One is our general and the other a black and white puppy. Stonewall, the puppy, travels everywhere with me and the troops. I even taught him how to stand at attention! During roll call, Stonewall stands straight and still, eyes front, with his paws at his side. During battle, the men put him in an ammunition box, so he won't get hurt. He barks like mad, wanting to get out and fight!—**Confederate Sergeant Van**

Shhh!

The Union sent us a new general all the way from the West. The first thing he did was stand before all of us who were weary from battle and make this speech: I have come from the West, where we have always seen the backs of our enemies. I presume that I have been called here to pursue the same system and to lead you against the enemy. My buddies were ready to shoot him down with their muskets, after that. How dare he mock us, saying we don't know how to pursue our enemies?! Who is he to change things here in Virginia? He hasn't seen a real battle until he fights it on our soil. I know one thing, he won't earn my respect until he's given me his!—**Union soldier** in the Army of Virginia under Gen. Pope

He is one of the only people in my life I can truly say I deeply dislike.—**Gen. Lee** about Gen. Pope

Woof! Woof!

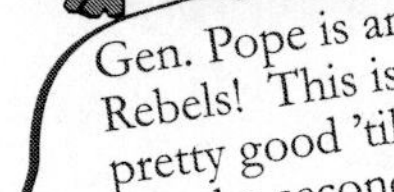

Gen. Pope is angry as an alligator! We strike back at those sneaky Rebels! This is our second battle at Manassas.. We were doin' pretty good 'til Gen. James Longstreet showed up, gol' darn him! For the second time we have been defeated at this place they call Bull Run.—**Union soldier**

He took charge of everything, commanding us this way and that. None of his strategies make sense. He rides around as if he knows everything about the battlefield at Manassas, but he knows nothing. He orders us to carry out impossible tasks during the battle. We are up against Gen. Lee and Stonewall Jackson, an intimidating pair, but Gen. Pope had no hesitation. If you ask me, he should have. Our defeat was swift and humiliating. Now he wants to blame his failure on us!—**commanding officer** under Gen. Pope

to owner…1858…Minnesota joins Union as free state…Illinois candidates Abraham Lincoln and Stephen Douglas debate issues of slavery; Douglas wins

demonstrate for equal rights in 100 cities, and over 3,600 are jailed...1963 …Dr. Martin Luther King, Jr., delivers his "I Have a Dream" speech…Gloria Richardson is the only black woman to lead a local civil rights group… Charlayne Hunter-Gault is

Antietam

Finally, we have no Union Army in Virginia! The time is ripe to invade the North on its own turf!—**Gen. Robert E. Lee**

Up rose old Barbara Frietchie then,
Bowed with her fourscore years and ten;

Bravest of all in Frederick town,
She took up the flag the men hauled down;

In her attic-window the staff she set,
to show that one heart was loyal yet...

Bloodiest of the War!

I'm just a poor farmer tryin' to get in the fall crops so these worn-out soldiers of ours can eat. Sure hope Gen. Lee and his troops can march on up and whack those Federals into surrender.—**Virginia farmhand**

Gen. McClellan,
My official orders are to take action. Gen. Lee's army is small in number and weak. If you attack, you can not only demand a retreat, but overcome the entire army post. In the past, you have hesitated to take your mighty Army of the Potomac into battle for fear of loss. But Sir, I must remind you, this is war! Casualties are inevitable. This fight is the Union's. You must act swiftly.
In deepest regard,
*President Abraham Lincoln**

*McClellan approached the battle at Antietam with confidence, but as he neared he began to suspect that Gen. Lee had more men. Although this was not so, McClellan gave Lee time to get his men ready. The battle is considered a "victory" for the Union, but President Lincoln was very upset by McClellan's weak attack.

Perhaps my greatest advantage is the delay of McClellan's troops. Though they are larger and better equipped, we continue to win battles over the Union on account of McClellan's leadership. We have only to wait on his hesitation, then attack!—**Gen. Robert E. Lee**

Wed., Sept. 17: Our army is divided already. Heard the enemy found Lee's battle orders, yet no sight of McClellan and his troops. No, I am wrong—here they appear along Antietam Creek. The sun is just rising. Better get my weary bones up—this is liable to be a day to remember?—**Confederate captain**

Yeehaaaa! What a wild battle! Instead of slamming all his troops at us, Gen. McClellan has made separate attacks, giving us a needed break. Gen. Lee shifts us back and forth. Sharpsburg, Dunkard Church, East Woods, Bloody Lane…I hardly know where I am. We are exhausted, confused, but we fight on! Our line almost broken, Gen. Ambrose Powell Hill's men rushed on the scene to hit hard Gen. Ambrose Burnside* at the bridge. Hope those great wads of whiskers on his cheeks go up in flames!—**Confederate soldier**

* Sideburns were named after Gen. Burnside because of his distinctive whiskers.

………we……..quit fightin'……..after 14 long hours ……it is dark……..I can't see ……..I can't hear……… ……I can't……..
—**soldier**

You're Fired!

At daybreak we assess the toll of battle: 4,800 dead, 18,500 wounded, many of which will surely die in our crude field hospitals. Those who can, limp away. No one won this battle. No one.*—**captain**

*Antietam was the single bloodiest day of the entire Civil War.

Well, you lost!

I have been relieved of my position as general of the Union troops. President Lincoln will undoubtedly struggle to fill my shoes. I expect to be called to return to command in little time. I am a man of destiny, and my destiny is to lead this Union to freedom and victory!—**Gen. McClellan***

* McClellan was never called upon to return to command of the Union Army. He ran for president in 1864, but did not win.

Lincoln thinks ending slavery will end the war. Will it?—**Edmond F.**, Maryland haberdasher

We are dying of thirst, fighting for water!—**soldier**

More than 7,600 killed at Perryville, all for naught!—**soldier**

Baton Rouge…Iuka…Newtonia…Corinth…Prairie Grove…

Shhh...

By the grace of God we've held off the Union troops in Virginia. It's been a long series of battles, but my men are fighting strong and we've had success. I try to keep my battle plans a secret, even to my commanders, until right before the fight. I want my men alert. The attack should be a swift, terrifying surprise for the enemy!—**Thomas "Stonewall" Jackson**

No! No!

I turned President Lincoln down twice before I took this commission to replace Gen. McClellan as commander of the Army of the Potomac. I knew I wasn't up to the job. I thought if I continued to send infantry to attempt to secure Fredericksburg for Union forces we would ultimately be successful. To God and the families of the dead, I ask forgiveness because my actions at Fredericksburg led to a slaughter of my men, even though we outnumbered Lee's army by over 20,000. I take full responsibility for the calamitous failure of my strategy and the suffering endured by these courageous and gallant soldiers.—**Gen. Ambrose Burnside**

That's nothin' more miserable than a soldier in snow…winter's comin' on… We are headed to Vicksburg…oh, woe is me…—**Union infantryman**

No one need kid themselves: though we tighten the noose, the South still fights hard.—**Gen. U.S. Grant**

Ah-hay! What's this? Our leisurely march through Mississippi finds us in a surprise attack at Holly Springs! Confederate horsemen have captured 4,000 soldiers…10,000 muskets, and destroyed our railroads and supplies!—**Union soldier**

Sir! News from Chickasaw Bayou! Gen. Sherman lost 1,800 men to the Rebel's 200!—**Union scout**

Sir! News from Fredericksburg! Gen. Burnside attacked 14 times! Says those Virginia hills just too well defended. Says here *We might as well have tried to take Hell!* 12,600 losses! Soldiers frozen where they fell. Sorry, Sir.—**Union messenger**

It is the last day of 1862. We are weary and cold here in Murfreesboro, Tennessee. Gen. William Starke Rosecrans and Gen. Bragg are duking it out. For three days we have been fighting mostly on open ground along Stones River. First the Feds are ahead, then the Rebs. Matters not, both sides beaten and battered, at least a third of each army lost.—**Nashville resident**

It is well that war is so terrible [otherwise] we should grow too fond of it.—**Gen. Robert E. Lee**

Charley, did I dream it?

Dream what?

That battle—why we were just a stone's throw from the enemy, remember? We sang, they sang, why we could hear each other's words.

Lotta blood.

Yeah. *Home, Sweet Home*, that's what they sang.

That's what we sang, too. Lotta dead.

Yeah.

Happy New Year, brother.

Yeah.

1863

LINCOLN SIGNS EMANCIPATION PROCLAMATION!

...all persons held as slaves within any State or designated part of a state the people whereof shall then be in rebellion against the United States, shall be then, thenceforward, and forever free...—**Abraham Lincoln**, from the Emancipation Proclamation

No far off president's goin' to free my slaves. He ain't got the right. Up there in his big ole house makin' decisions for the lot of us. Well, I ain't listenin' cause he ain't my president no more. I'm part of the Confederacy now. I'll listen to President Davis alone. My slaves'll just stay right where they're at, ain't goin' nowhere. None of them's free, not till I say so.—**plantation owner**

I'm on my way to our nation's capital, Washington, D.C. I heard there's black refugees from the South come to live in D.C. to escape the war. I've got to help them! What soldiers and politicians forget is that people have to keep on livin' once all this fightin's over. How's a black slave gonna find work, or a home? My plan is to convince Northern businessmen to hire these newly freed black men and women. They're good workers, all of 'em. Once they have a job, we'll find 'em a place to live, maybe even out West. All I know is, if it's up to me, blacks are gonna have a good life livin' free.—**Sojourner Truth**

Lot's of folks around here don't think it's right for a black man to fight in the war. But that wasn't stopping me. I rounded up as many able-bodied Louisiana men as I could find to help me fight. We all want our part in ending slavery once and for all. We're a group of all black soldiers and I'm the only black captain in the whole state of Louisiana!—**P.B.S. Pinchback**

I am so frustrated! We have given those Union boys a terrible whipping here near Murfreesboro, but they won't give up. I had felt victory within my grasp, but it slips away.—**Gen. Braxton Bragg**

Did ya' hear? Old Burnside is bein' hung out to dry! They're replacin' him with General "Fightin' Joe" Hooker. Now, we'll show those Rebels!—**Union soldier**

It was such a thrill to help out my side in the war. I was out in the field when Confederate troops galloped to me and asked if there was any way to cross the river near my house. The Yankees had crossed before them and burned the bridge. I jumped on my horse and led them through the woods to a safe crossing. They defeated the Yankees that day and gave me a gold medal for helping!—**Emma Sansom**, 16

I have the finest army on the planet. I have the finest army the sun ever shone on. If the enemy does not run, God help them. May God have mercy on General Lee, for I will have none.—**Union Gen, Joseph Hooker** before the Battle of Chancellorsville

John Henry Johnson reporting for duty, Sir! I walked all the way from Salem to Boston, and I'm ready to fight for this great Union. Let me be a part of the 54th regiment of colored men and I surely won't let you down!—**John Henry Johnson**, 16

"Fightin' Joe Hooker" won't fight! He's lost his nerve. We're runnin'. Get back to the old Chancellor house at the crossroads. How did this happen? **— Union soldier**

Hooker may have 134,000 men here at Chancellorsville, Virginia, but he underestimates Gen. Lee and his 60,000! Lee's gonna' use the same tactic he did at the Second Battle of Manassas. Divide his troops. He's leavin' a few to fight at Fredericksburg and takin' the rest with Stonewall Jackson to sneak up and attack Hooker's unprotected right flank from the rear.—**Confederate newspaper reporter**

Nobody wants to camp at the old Bull Run Battlefield. I hear that place is haunted! My knees shook when my sergeant ordered I stand night guard. I was standing in the rain, when lightning lit up the sky. I spotted small, white shapes moving quickly. It had to be the ghosts! But when I peeked between my fingers, I saw that the shapes weren't ghosts—just sheep!—**Isaac Scherich**

It was dark. The only thing I could see were shadows and outlines. We've been out here fightin' like this for days. I know it's no excuse but I was exhausted. My eyes failed me. I thought it was the enemy. A Union escort, maybe, fired: one, two, three. BANG, BANG, BANG. I heard a scream. Someone shouted "General Jackson, someone shot General Jackson!" He had three gunshot wounds in his arm. What have I done?—**Confederate soldier***

*Just days after the gunshot wound to his arm, Thomas "Stonewall" Jackson died.

Let us cross over the river, and rest under the shade of the trees…—**Thomas "Stonewall" Jackson's** final words

I've lost my right arm. My heart is bleeding.—**Robert E. Lee** on "Stonewall" Jackson's death

Word just came Gen. Jackson has been shot. Gen. Lee asked me to take his place mid-battle. I have become the leader of Virginia's 2nd Corps in just a few short hours! The battle is raging, the men disheartened because of their wounded leader. They're expecting me to rise up. And I must, for these soldiers… HOLD STEADY, MEN! "REMEMBER JACKSON!"—**J.E.B. Stuart**

I hear the Union army suffered more than 17,000 casualties and the Confederates lost about 13,000. The Battle of Chancellorsville might be General Lee's greatest victory – he's put that great Army of the Potomac on the defensive – but he lost Stonewall. That hurts.—**citizen of Fredericksburg**

Hooker, You're Fired!

Hooker made excuses about our loss at Chancellorsville, but President Lincoln booted him, anyways. We got us a new commander of the Army of the Potomac—General George Meade.—**Union soldier**

I never thought I'd see Ambrose Burnside again—especially after I left him at the altar! Poor soul should have known I'd be a runaway bride. Why, all at the same time, I'd been engaged to 12 men, and my sister Ginnie, to 15 men! The two of us are always searching for adventure—that's why we became spies for the Confederate army! Unfortunately, a Union soldier found 50 letters in our trunk, and we were arrested. Wish me luck!—**Lottie Moon**

I loved that man! He was a Rebel, tried and true. I get teary-eyed when I think about that dreadful battle at Gettysburg. I was nursing sick and wounded Confederate soldiers when I heard my sweetheart had taken a bullet and died. It was then I decided that I wanted to do more for my state. I became North Carolina's most famous spy! These full skirts aren't just for looks—they're real nice for hiding secret documents, as well. When those Yanks finally caught me, I swallowed the top secret message I was carrying right then and there! I'm returning to my home in North Carolina now. I won't be in prison too long. The soldiers will let me go without even having a trial! After all, who can resist the charm of a Southern Belle?—**Emmeline Piggott**

It's 'bout time we moved into Yankee territory. Lee is takin' us straight to Washington. We'll show everyone around the world what we're made of. We'll take this fight onto Yankee soil and whip 'em!—**Confederate soldier**

D.C.

Charge!!! Sabers flash! Pistols ring! These Yankee Cavalry aren't half bad. Better than we expected. But here at Brandy Station, our 10,000 will beat their 10,000. It will be the greatest cavalry battle ever fought on American soil! Charge!!!—**Confederate Cavalry Officer**

First, we broke away from the Confederate state of Virginia. And now, the great state of West Virginia has been granted statehood in the glorious United States of America!—**statesman from West Virginia**

Vicksburg, Mississippi, is the key to victory in the Western Theater of this war! It's the last outpost preventing our control of the Mississippi River. If we take Vicksburg, we'll cut the Confederacy in half at the river, isolating Texas, Arkansas and Missouri and prevent them from providing any support to Richmond. It must be controlled!—**Union Senator**

Even after sundown, guns are still being fired. The Confederates of Vicksburg refuse to surrender. We have been fighting for over a month and a half. Conditions are bad. The citizens have no food and have resorted to eating rats! I do hope this battle will soon be won by the mighty Union army.—**Captain William T. House**

Those batt'ries were high up on those bluffs at Vicksburg, guardin' that river. Admiral Porter moved our gunboats downriver past those batt'ries night after night without much damage. They never suspicioned that we were gettin' in position to move Grant's Army across the Mississippi just south of 'em. No one expected Grant to cut himself off from his supplies. But, dang! it was a brilliant move!—**Confederate gunboatman**

Run for cover!

We've abandoned the supply line, Gen. Grant, sir. All troops are carryin' three days rations and then they'll live off the land if they have to. We're prepared to move at lightnin' speed!—**Union sergeant**

We're trapped and outnumbered two to one, General! Grant's and Sherman's troops are all around us. All we can do is make it to Vicksburg with the men who are left and try to defend ourselves.—**Confederate Officer**

Bob's my uncle!

Uncle!

Shells have been bombardin' Vicksburg for uncountable days, now. Our citizens are livin' in caves and dugouts to protect themselves, and we are starvin'—our food nearly gone. Sickness is spreadin' throughout this swelterin' Mississippi heat. Surely, no people in this terrible war have suffered as much as we have.—**Vicksburg mother**

Gen. Pemberton has surrendered. Vicksburg has fallin' into the hands of the enemy. They control the Mississippi River, and the Confederacy is fightin' for survival!—**Confederate statesman**

officially begins...Federal Navy blockades Southern ports...Virginia, Arkansas, North Carolina, and Tennessee join Confederacy...Union defeated at Battle of

York elects Shirley Chisholm as first African American U.S. Congresswoman...1969...Mary Moultrie leads a wage strike at the Medical College Hospital in South Carolina...1972... Political activist and intellectual, Angela Davis is acquitted of murder

Where is Jeb Stuart and his cavalry? He is Gen. Lee's eyes and ears. We have 70,000 troops movin' into Pennsylvania, but we have no idea where the Army of the Potomac is. Gen. Lee says to head to the little crossroads town of Gettysburg!—**aide to General Lee**

Teacher said we were going on a field trip to meet real, live Union soldiers! They were camped right outside our schoolhouse waiting for the Rebels to march up on them. The morning of our field trip, we woke up to cannon booms and gunshots. The Rebels were already there and a battle was on! Before I knew it, they were fighting in our school yard and the schoolhouse became a Yankee hospital! I even helped give medicine to those poor, hurt men!—**student of Carrie Sheads**

Union cavalry is waitin' at Gettysburg! Attack!!—**Confederate infantryman**

Where is Stuart!? I need him. He's my eyes and ears. My men are dying. Where is Stuart?? He should have been here a day ago… God help us.—**Robert E. Lee** on J.E.B. Stuart's late arrival to the Battle of Gettysburg

Look Out!

We're pushin' those Yanks back through the streets of Gettysburg all the way back to Cemetery Ridge! Keep 'em comin' boys, we got 'em outnumbered. What? We're not gonna' attack again? But they got the high ground!—**Confederate Captain**

When this battle at Gettysburg began, I had only been in command of the Army of the Potomac for three days. Today, it feels like three years. We were victorious and have kept Gen. Lee from pushing northward, but the toll is heavy. Everywhere I look, I see the bodies of brave young men, both from my army and from the army of my enemy. There could be 50,000 perished; there could be more. We must bury them with honor, and move on.—**Gen. George Meade**

We are sopping with sweat and blood…my ears and eyes sting from the never-ending hissin, shriek, and roar that envelops us. The summer heat is unbearable. My skin feels on fire and my thirst overwhelms me. Yet we have confidence in Gen. Meade. He continues to move us around to shore up weak points in our lines. But look! The rebels are charging! WATCH OUT!—**Union soldier**

All night long, those Yanks been diggin' up there. Ya' can hear the scrapes of those shovels and axes. They gettin' dug in good on that ridge. And that ain't good for us.—**Confederate soldier**

The Rebels are charging' up Little Round Top Hill. We can't loose it or the whole Union line will be open to attack. Whoever controls this hill, controls the battlefield. Fight hard, men!—**Union captain**

Gen. Meade, sir. All lines are holding. Little Round Top and Culp's Hill. We've lost a lot of men, but our positions are strong for another day.—**aide**

I don't know what possessed her to do it. Thinking back now, I should have stopped Jennie. It was the second day of the battle at Gettysburg. The troops were firing right next to our house, it seemed. Most of the neighbors had fled to somewhere safer, but my oldest daughter was weak from having just delivered a child. We decided to move my oldest daughter and her baby to the cellar to keep her safe. I was tending to her, but Jennie was upstairs. I was so caught up in taking care of her older sister, I didn't think to tell Jennie to come down to safety. Suddenly, I heard a loud BOOM, then a scream…I ran upstairs to find Jennie laying on the kitchen floor, lifeless…wet bread dough was sitting on the counter…in shock, all I could do was finish baking the bread. My sweet daughter, just a young teenager, was bravely making it for the soldiers, I couldn't let her down.—**Jennie Wade's mother**

Pointing a gun at the head of the leader of that gang of Rebels, I said, "Come on in, if you want to; some of you shall fall, or I will!" They said they would kill me if I did not put down the gun, but I answered, "The first man of you that takes a step towards this door dies. This is the home of my parents, my brothers and sisters, and I am able to, and shall, defend it."—**Miss Schwartz**, 15-years-old

Bull Run—first official battle of the Civil War…1862…1st ironclad ship battle between Monitor and Merrimac…2nd Battle of Bull Run ends in Union defeat

in a political trial in California… Equal Employment Opportunity Act passes…1974…The Coalition of Labor Union Women is formed…1978…U.S. Postal Service issues a Black Heritage postage stamp series…1983…Martin Luther King, Jr. Day is

Ol' Lee has hit our flanks and not done the job. Today, he'll come at our center. You can bet on that!—**Union infantryman**

Jeb Stuart and the cavalry has at last arrived. They'll attack the Union rear. Gen. Ewell will attack Culp's Hill. Once the cannon attack is over, Gen. Pickett's division will march straight across the field and into the middle of the Union line at Cemetery Ridge. Godspeed, men!—**Confederate captain**

President Davis has denied my request for resignation from the Confederate Army command. He wants me to fight this war through until its end, but I don't know if I can continue. Because of my decisions, thousands of men lost their lives. A bloody field now marks their graves. Sons, brothers, fathers, all dead. How much longer can this devastating war continue?—**Robert E. Lee**

Four score and seven yeas ago our fathers brought forth on this continent a new nation, conceived in Liberty, and dedicated to the proposition that all men are created equal…and that government of the people, by the people, for the people, shall not perish from the earth.—**Abraham Lincoln**, from the Gettysburg Address

Play ball!

The prisoners nearly every day are engaged in a game they call 'base-ball'…I don't understand the game, as there is a great deal of running and little apparent gain, but those who play it get very excited over it.—**John Delhaney**, teenage Confederate soldier captured at the battle of Gettysburg and sent to Fort Henry

I may be beautiful, but trust me, I got a temper. I once shot a Federal soldier just because he insulted my momma. I think I'm just as brave as any soldier boy! I get my information by flirting or eavesdropping. I once ran through an open, raging battlefield to give Stonewall Jackson his information. I've been arrested seven times and imprisoned twice. But that won't stop me. Once, I even hid secret information in a rubber ball and tossed it through my jail cell window to a Southern admirer below.—**Belle Boyd**

So I walked my army out of Chattanooga and practically handed it to the Federals on a silver platter! They won't stay there long. I'll spread the rumor that my army is breakin' up, and they'll come after me here at Chickamauga, thinkin' I'm an easy target. Gen. Longstreet's 12,000 men are nearly here. Then, I'll have close to 72,000 men, and the Army of the Cumberland will be nearly as large as Lee's army at Gettysburg. We'll outnumber Rosecrans's Federal troops by 10,000 soldiers.—**Gen. Braxton Bragg**

I hope he can hold those yankees until I get there!

Retreat! Retreat!! Sound the retreat! Longstreet's men have broken through a gap in our front line. They've overrun Gen. Rosecrans's headquarters. Half the army is retreating back to Chattanooga! —**Union soldier**

Gen. Thomas refuses to retreat. He's forming a line of defense on the ridge of Snodgrass Hill. Those Rebels will be coming at him with all they've got!—**Union captain**

They keep comin'. We keep shootin'. The carnage is sickening. How many boys have to die before they stop coming at us?—**soldier**

Our losses are great on both sides. This fight is futile. When night falls, we'll retreat to Chattanooga and join Gen. Rosecrans and the rest of the army. Let Bragg have this one.—Union **Gen. George H. Thomas**

The U.S. Sanitary Commission funds were running low. As creator, I needed to do something big to keep the organization going. We decided to host a fair which had never been done before. We would have a parade, exhibits, and an auction of the real Emancipation Proclamation signed by President Lincoln himself! We hoped to raise $25,000, a fair sum. But when we counted the money, we had almost raised $100,000—more than enough to keep the Sanitary Commission going. I couldn't believe it!—**Jane Hoge**

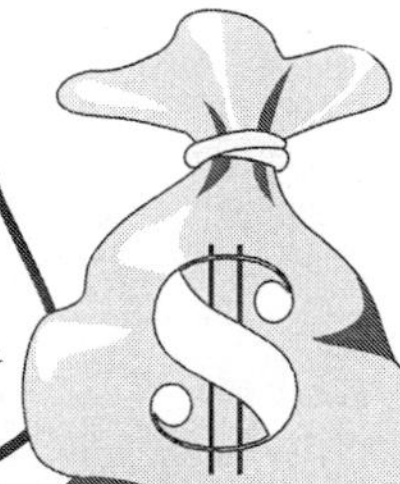

Often at midnight I find myself sittin' next to the cot of some poor boy who's about to enter the Vast Unknown. I find myself cryin' for him and for the mother who cannot be here beside him. I spend my days nursin' them—there have been hundreds, maybe thousands, of 'em. But at night, I mend the blue regulation pants or the frock of some neglected soldier boy, or darn a pile of socks, singin' softly "Home, Sweet Home," or "We Are Coming Father Abraham."—**Mrs. Sturgis**, a nurse known as Mother by Union troops

War is killing, and the way to kill is to get there first with the most men.—**Gen. Nathan Bedford Forrest**

I may not have as much experience as the generals down here, but one thing I know—war's for fightin'! If you don't have the courage to face the enemy head-on, then you don't have the courage to be in this war. I've overcome an enemy of 2,000 men with less than 1,000 on my side. If the Confederacy wants to win, we got to keep on fightin', no matter what.—**Gen. Nathan Bedford Forrest**

That man's become a thorn in my side. He spends his time leading his measly group of men in meaningless attack after attack. We spend our days fixing the damage he creates. My immediate orders are to have Forrest stopped for good! He's just a headache.—**Union commander**

For nearly two months now Chattanooga, Tennessee, has been under siege. The Rebels are entrenched on Lookout Mountain and along Missionary Ridge with their cannons pointed straight at us. Their cavalry is destroyin' the supply trains tryin' to get through. We are hungry and sick of war. When will this ever end?—**Union medic**

I will hold this town till we starve.—**Union Gen. George H. Thomas**

Gen. Grant, Fightin' Joe Hooker, and Gen. Sherman have all come to Chattanooga. We are bustin' out of here!—**Union soldier**

We don't need orders! Take Missionary Ridge! Chickamauga! Chickamauga! Remember Chickamauga! Those Rebs won't beat us again!—**Union infantryman**

My, God, we're helpless! Yankees are runnin' up Missionary Ridge so fast. If we fire at the enemy, we hit our own men retreating. Break ranks and run, run for your lives!—**Confederate cannoneer**

We own Tennessee! Go after them, Gen. Sherman. We're gonna' chase those Rebels all the way into Georgia.—**Gen. Ulysses S. Grant**

What do they want from me? I gave them victory at Chickamauga, and now they criticize me after things went badly in Chattanooga? Some have called me a brilliant strategist. Others say I hesitate, that I don't take advantage of opportunities. I say not!—**Gen. Braxton Bragg**

We started out strong. Our victories at Fort Sumter and the Battle of Bull Run had the men confident that this war was ours. But then we lost Gettysburg, Vicksburg, and Richmond. A lot of men died. Morale is low. I'm headed to Georgia to try to encourage the troops. The war is not over and neither are we. —**Jefferson Davis**

War Department establishes Bureau of Colored Troops...Confederate General Thomas "Stonewall" Jackson killed... Grant conquers Vicksburg, Mississippi

becomes the first African American female U.S. astronaut...1993...Toni Morrison becomes first African American female to win a Pulitzer Prize in literature for her novel, Beloved...2000...President George W. Bush appoints African American

1864

The Union army has been squabbling to find the right direction for months. McClellan was a disaster. I've gone through countless generals. What I need is true leadership. My main goal is to defeat Gen. Lee, the Confederacy's one remaining strong point. I think I have found just the right person for the job. He's unknown around here, his name is Ulysses S. Grant.—**President Lincoln**

Gen. Grant's got a new plan to organize the Union armies across the North under one war strategy. No other general has been able to make sense out of this mess of a war. I hope Grant is different.—**Union soldier**

Things are fixin' to get hot!

My war strategy is simple: fight the Confederates until they cease to exist! Don't let them rest. Don't let them escape. Everywhere those Rebels turn, the Union will be waiting.—**Gen. Grant**

My biggest enemy now is General Ulysses S. Grant.— **Gen. Lee**

I am setting out with Gen. Meade at my side toward the Army of Virginia. My plan is to overwhelm the Rebels with force on all sides. We will fight until they are weak with surrender.—**Gen. Grant**

No Confederates Allowed!

There's about no food left and we've lost more men than I can count. But when it came time to reenlist in these here Confederate troops, I didn't hesitate one second. I'm a man who'll fight this war to its end…and come out winnin'.—**Confederate soldier**

Military outposts report Grant is leading his troops south through the Virginia wilderness toward the Army of Northern Virginia.—**Confederate messenger**

I've heard reports that Grant is headed south. That means we're headed north, men. This is Virginia, our land. We'll meet him head-on and have the advantage of knowing our way around this territory.—**Gen. Lee**

Gen. Grant marches us troops through the Virginia wilderness south of Richmond. The brown, dry grass crunches beneath my boots. Our supply wagons are tangled in undergrowth, and we can hardly see for the tall pines. I'm terrified a Confederate musket will point out from behind one of these trees and aim at me! I feel like an easy target.—**Union soldier**

How can we fight in this tangled mass of woods in the wilderness of Virginia? The brush and trees are so thick we cannot move, we cannot see, we stumble into our enemies in this choking fog. I fear the worst when the smoke clears.—**Gen. George Meade**

I was so terrified of being shot by a Rebel that my commander looked at me and said, *Nonsense, they couldn't hit an elephant from here.* Just as he said it, a bullet struck him and he fell off his horse, dead!—**Union soldier** describing Commander John Sedgwick's death

CONFEDERATES!!! Take aim, men!—**Union commander**

I look up from battle for a moment and am struck at the confusion of the troops. Men fight in small groups all over the place. The woods are so choked with smoke, it's impossible to see right in front of my face. It looks more like grown men fighting a bully than a battle.—**Confederate soldier**

Cannons are no good in these thick woods. We've resorted to shooting our rifles only. Gunpowder sparked a raging forest fire. As the sun sets, I hear men…our own soldiers…screaming for their lives, burning to death, and there is nothing I can do.—**Union commander**

…Union gains control of Mississippi River…West Virginia joins Union as free state…Battle of Gettysburg begins to turn tide of war for Union… Lincoln gives

Condoleezza Rice to serve as his U.S. National Security Advisor…2002…Tiger Woods becomes the youngest golfer (age 26!) to win 8 PGA major titles… African American tennis star Serena Williams wins the U.S. Open and Wimbledon

UNION TROOPS MAKE STRONG COMEBACK IN THE BATTLE OF THE WILDERNESS, CONFEDERATES WEAKENED!—newspaper headline

While my men celebrate what they think is victory, I am somber. We made little progress against the Union today. All we have to show are 10,000 casualties for the South alone. I cannot imagine how many fine young men the Union has lost tonight.—**Gen. Lee**

We took 'em Yanks by surprise. You shoulda seen the looks on their faces when we marched up on 'em. Terrified of a bunch of old farmers! Gen. Lee ordered we're gonna continue fightin' in the wilderness till it's won. No doubt in my mind, Confederates'll win this battle.—**Confederate soldier**

If Grant's like any other Yankee general he'll retreat and attack us later…like a coward!—**Confederate soldier**

CONFEDERATE TROOPS PUSH BACK UNION AT THE BATTLE OF THE WILDERNESS IN A BRAVE DISPLAY OF STRENGTH!—newspaper headline

When we arrived at the Spotsylvania Court House, the Rebels were hunkered down in breastworks* with their rifles, waiting for our arrival.—**Union soldier**

breastworks: low walls built to protect troops

You men may be used to running away with your tail tucked between your legs, but you've got a new general now. We're not letting those Rebels out of our sight. We'll follow them to Spotsylvania and all over the south, until they're weakened…even if it takes all summer!—**Gen. Grant**

I saw them march across the field early one morning. The Yankees have finally made it to Petersburg. My orders are to guard this city with my life, and that's what I'll do. I am outnumbered, my 2,200 men to 15,000 Union troops, but I will protect this city as best I can until Lee arrives with the rest of the troops.—**Gen. P.G.T. Beauregard**

We have fought bitterly for weeks. Grant pushed my army all over Virginia. Now, I know right where he's leading his troops…Petersburg!—**Gen. Lee**

No ground made today. The Rebels' determination makes up for their lack in numbers. They are weak, but will not give up. Lee is a brave and fierce opponent. He has the respect of his men.—**Gen. Grant**

Well I thought I'd never see the day when the Union threatened to take everything we have from us. There they are, waitin' on the outskirts of town to take us over. If they gain Petersburg, that's it for the Confederacy…at least for Virginia. Petersburg is where all the railroads come together. It's the lifeline of the Confederate Army. Without these trains, no one in the South can get supplies, food, nothin'. We'd have to abandon Richmond, our capital, and find another place to survive. I pray the good Lord sends his help.—**Petersburg housewife**

Lee arrived today. I feel I can breath a sigh of relief.—**Gen. Beauregard**

It's a miracle we've held back the Yankees this long. Each time they charge our trench, we fire at them with everything we've got…bayonets, knives, even tin cans!—**citizen of Petersburg**, temporary volunteer Confederate soldier

Guess boredom has a way of makin' men stupid. The Yanks came up with a "brilliant" plan to blow a hole in the field right under us Confederates. They got coal miners to dig a path underground and plant explosives under our feet. Only problem was, when the bombs went off and the ground blew up, the Union soldiers just marched toward us and jumped in the hole! What were they thinkin'?! We walked right up to the 30 foot deep hole, pointed our guns down at those poor, stupid Yanks and fired away. They were lined up like cows in a slaughter house.—**Confederate soldier**

Pee-yew!

All we've done for days is stare at those ugly Rebels. They stink, too! Lee and Grant ordered a siege. Nobody is fighting until the other is ready to give up their position. I'm starting to go stir-crazy with boredom!—**Union soldier**

The siege continues. No telling how long we must sit in this field and stare at each other while our guns collect dust.—**Union soldier**

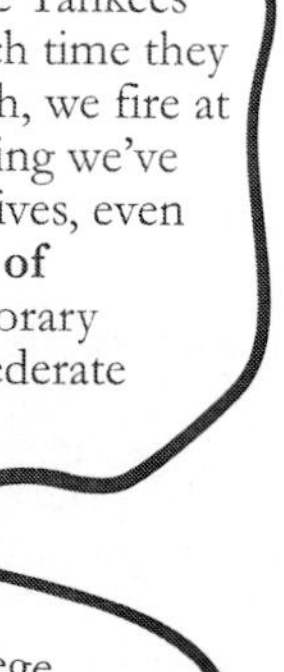

You can imagine my surprise as a Southern gentlewoman when an unknown black man came knockin' at my door. I opened it slowly, suspiciously. He opened his mouth, all of a sudden like, and pulled out a piece of tin foil. He slowly unraveled the foil with his fingers to reveal a sheet of fine paper with a note written on it. It was from Gen. Sheridan of the Union troops. He asked for any information I knew about the Confederate Army. I hate slavery and secretly support the Union. So, I wrote my reply on the tissue paper and watched the man stuff it back in his mouth. My neighbors would be appalled to know I'm aiding the Union Army!—**Rebecca Wright**

Today I set off southward into the Confederate state of Georgia to push back Rebel troops and end this war once and for all. My opponent is the smart, but hardly aggressive Gen. Johnston.—**Union Gen. William Tecumseh Sherman**

That Jeff Davis doesn't know what it's like to be out here on the field. He sits up in the capital making war decisions from his comfortable office. He wants me to take an offensive march on Chattanooga. But if I send troops there, no one will be left to protect Atlanta. He may be president of this Confederacy, but I'm general of the Army of Tennessee and I've got to go by my own orders in this war!—**Gen. Joseph E. Johnston**

UNION AND CONFEDERATE TROOPS FIGHT THROUGH GEORGIA FOR CONTROL OF ATLANTA!

Gen. Sherman has to fight like he's got one arm tied behind his back. He's got to stay close to the North Georgia railroad supply line that brings us food and supplies. We need about 14,000 tons of supplies each day! That means we can't attack anything that's more than a day's march away from the railroad.—**Union soldier**

I only have to hold back Sherman long enough to get us through the election. If the Union sees two of their top generals at a standstill in Virginia and Georgia, they'll lose faith in their beloved Lincoln. Once a new president comes into power, the Union will be forced to make peace. My battle plan is to stall the Yankees.—**Gen. Johnston**

Our first encounter with the Yankees was in the foothills of the Appalachians. I was ready to fight, but not for what I saw. Soldier after soldier came marching toward us. While we were busy fightin' half of them, the other half marched right around us! We have no defense against this huge army.—**Confederate soldier**

Listen up, men! Gen. Johnston has his troops ready for battle at Allatoona, Georgia. I've been there. The Rebels will have advantage if we attack. They expect us to come after them because we have a supply train that runs through that area. But I won't risk defeat. So, gather all the supplies you can. Load them into the wagons, then follow me. Those are orders!—**Gen. Sherman**

Seems like we keep retreating. I sure hope Gen. Johnston's got a plan up his sleeve.—**Confederate soldier**

After two months of trekking across Georgia, it looks like we'll spend more months in a siege over this town.—**Union soldier**

YANKEE TROOPS ARRIVE AT OUTSKIRTS OF ATLANTA

President Lincoln,
This is the official field report for the Atlanta Campaign. While Sherman has reached the outskirts of Atlanta, a long siege is expected. Sherman has lost about 17,000 men and had no full victory in any battle. Delegates fear that another long siege like the one in Petersburg could ruin your chances for reelection.—**Union messenger**

President Davis,
This is the official report for the Atlanta Campaign. Johnston has preserved most of the men in his army. However, they have been pushed back from north Georgia and now face Sherman at the outskirts of Atlanta. Most of his battles have ended in retreat.—**Confederate messenger**

That stubborn man! He has not followed one order I've given since the beginning of this God-forsaken Atlanta Campaign. He insisted on a defensive role, and look where he's gotten us…right down to Atlanta. I want Gen. Johnston removed from his position!—**Confederate President Jefferson Davis**

Johnston, You're Fired!

I appoint John B. Hood as General over the Army of Tennessee. He will relieve Gen. Johnston of all his previous duties.—**Jefferson Davis**

Gen. Sherman's plan is to take over the three railroad lines that run through Atlanta. Once we have control of them, the city is at our fingertips. We control everything that goes in and out.—**Union soldier**

It seems the Rebels have no clue that Sherman is marching us south around the city. No one is trying to stop us. Once we reach Jonesboro, we'll have control of the third and last rail line into the city and Atlanta will be ours!—**Union soldier**

The Rebels made it almost too easy for me. Gen. Hood is more incompetent than I expected. As he celebrated the Confederate's victory in taking Atlanta, my troops slipped past him. By the time he realized we were attacking, it was too late. My troops pushed up from Jonesboro and took Atlanta. My official report to Washington is as follows: *Atlanta is ours, and fairly won.*—**Gen. Sherman**

YANKEE CANNON SHOTS HEARD AROUND ATLANTA!

…Maryland abolishes slavery…Nevada joins union as free state…Abraham Lincoln wins reelection as president…Sherman begins "March to the Sea" through

Coordinating Committee, led by prominent African American lawyers and activists, announce plans to sue companies that profited from slavery… President George W. Bush awards comedian and actor Bill Cosby and baseball player Hank Aaron

I can no longer deny that I have lost the city of Atlanta to the Yankees. At my final attempt to salvage any Confederate dignity, I destroyed a rolling mill and 81 boxcars loaded with ammunition. The explosion should warn Atlanta citizens that Sherman has taken the city and they should evacuate as soon as possible. God help us.—**Gen. Hood**

War is cruelty, and you cannot refine it.—**Gen. Sherman** to the mayor of Atlanta

What I know are the facts: 80,000 of Grant's men dead so far. None of us are safe from the tragedy of this war. Yet, with all the sacrifice, Grant is still in Virginia, staring down the Confederates in a siege. Thanks to Lincoln, this war is accomplishing nothing.—**war-weary Northerner**

They don't call it Hotlanta for nothing!

We have chosen former Gen. McClellan to run against Lincoln in this election. He says he will fight to end this war peacefully, so he's got the Democratic vote!—**McClellan supporter**

That Lincoln is the worst president this Union has ever seen. Our country is ravaged by war because of his foolish decisions. He'll surely go down in history as one of America's worst presidents!—**dissatisfied Northerner**

Sherman has taken Atlanta! Perhaps there is progress in this war. Once the North wins and slavery is abolished we can live in peace again. Thanks to President Lincoln, the Union can almost taste victory. Lincoln's got my vote!—**Lincoln supporter**

Vote for Honest Abe!

LINCOLN WINS BY A LANDSLIDE!

This year marks my reelection as President of the United States. What a weary and strange job it has become. I am loved and hated by many. My party insists we fight this war until the end. Unconditional surrender, I once heard it said. The Union's goal is to first win, then end slavery, and reunite this Union. I pray the next four years have a brighter future than the past.—**Abraham Lincoln**

Now that I've taken Atlanta, I have but two choices before me: pursue and destroy Hood's army, or march south and destroy the Confederacy's ability to make war…I believe Gen. Hood will just have to wait...MEN, let's march toward the sea!—**Gen. Sherman**

Head onward to Nashville, men! We'll cut off the Yankee supply line and weaken those soldiers. They'll have to come after us and we'll be waiting. This war is not over yet!—**Gen. Hood**

I figured we would follow Hood's army north to Nashville, but Gen. Sherman had other plans. We're heading south! Sherman ordered us to march in one straight line, 60 miles wide, right through Georgia. We won't need supplies from Nashville because we're going to live off the land around us.—**Union soldier**

I heard so many footsteps it sounded like a wild stampede! I peeked out my front door and there they were, the Union army, marching in a line as far as my eye could see. I knew then we were lost. The Union had made it to South Georgia.—**Georgia grandmother**

Men, the sad truth is, we are simply outnumbered. Sherman's troops are storming through Georgia. To fight back with only 8,000 men is a death warrant. Those who can fight, fight! But know when to accept defeat gracefully.—**commander of the Georgia militia**

Sherman's troops have no respect for nothin' and no rules. They've been destroyin' everything in their path. They leave women an' chilen's cold and starved for the winter. They say they're destroyin' things for war, but this ain't war no more…this is down right cruelty.—**Georgia farmer**

Ma'am, I have official orders from Gen. Sherman that the Union Army can take whatever they need, or want, from your house and property. Please step aside.—**Union soldier**

Georgia…1865…Robert E. Lee appointed general-in-chief of all Confederate armies…Missouri abolishes slavery…Abraham Lincoln rejects Jefferson Davis's

the nation's highest civilian honor—the Presidential Medal of Freedom… 2005… Condoleezza Rice is appointed Secretary of State becoming the first African American woman to serve as Secretary of State…Hurricane Katrina hits southern coast

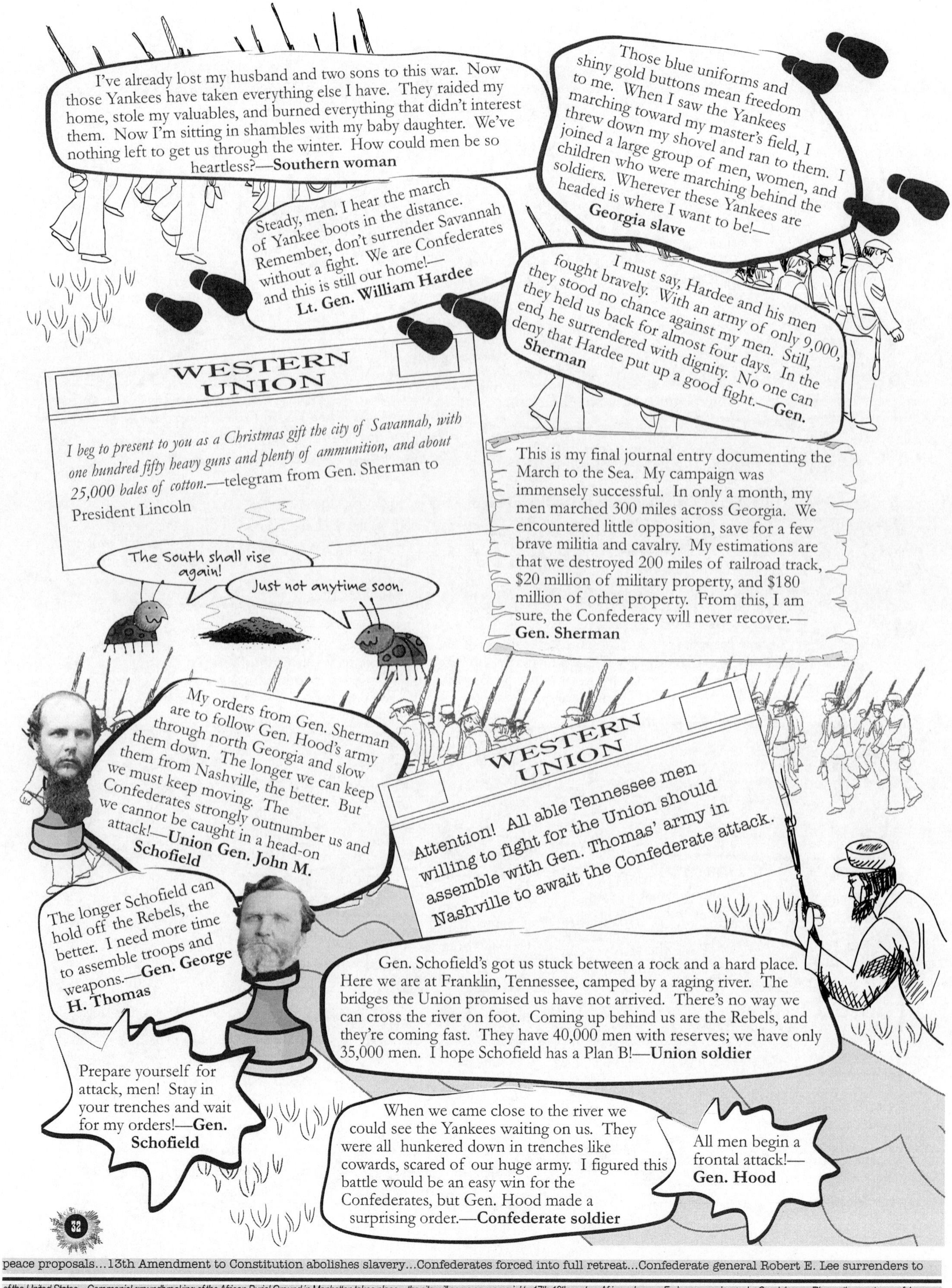

peace proposals...13th Amendment to Constitution abolishes slavery...Confederates forced into full retreat...Confederate general Robert E. Lee surrenders to

of the United States...Ceremonial groundbreaking of the African Burial Ground in Manhattan takes place—the site will serve as memorial to 17th-18th century African slaves...Forbes magazine ranks Condoleezza Rice as the most powerful

Half of our army wasn't even to the river yet. Cannons weren't set up. We had no artillery, just half our army with some wooden guns!—**Confederate soldier**

CHARGE!!! —**Gen. Hood**

I ran toward the Union trenches, confused by Gen. Hood's orders. I fired my gun. They fired back. Men all around me fell to the ground. The Union is winning!—**Confederate soldier**

Third Corps, INTO THE TRENCHES!—**Gen. Hood**

After all day fighting, and losing, Gen. Hood forced the Third Corps into the trenches with the Yankees. They didn't stand a chance. It was a senseless assault.—**Confederate soldier**

Rest tonight, men. In the morning, we'll attack with cannons and give those Yankees a rude awakening! —**Gen. Hood**

Ya snooze, Ya lose!

When I woke up, I headed directly to my cannon post. We began firing with all our artillery on the trenches in front of us. Suddenly Gen. Hood yelled CEASE FIRE!—**Confederate soldier**

We are shooting at dirt! The Union army escaped across the river during the night. We were fooled!—**Confederate soldier**

It sure is quiet now!

President Davis,
I regret to report that over 6,000 of my men died on the field at Franklin today. I lost 53 commanders as well. My army is weakened in strength and leadership. However, we will continue to pursue Nashville and I am confident we will see a Confederate victory.
Sincerely,
Gen. Hood

War is not about who gets there first, it's about who wins, and I plan to win this battle at Nashville. I won't attack the Confederates until I have all details in order. I must be absolutely sure of victory!— **Gen. Thomas**

Gen. Hood must have learned his lesson from the disaster in Franklin. We arrived in Nashville today and were ordered to wait outside the city walls until the Union attacks us. Doesn't sound like much of a plan to me, but what other option does Gen. Hood have?—**Confederate commander**

Today is the day, men, we have waited long enough. All details are in order. All you have to do is fight. We will attack the Confederates with as much force as possible. On my order, FIRE!— **Gen. Thomas**

They've been staring at each other for two weeks! Why hasn't Thomas attacked the Confederates? I can't imagine what he's waiting for, but he's waited long enough. We can't have two armies in siege at Nashville and Petersburg, it's bad for politics! Gen. Logan, travel to Nashville and relieve Gen. Thomas of his command. Then lead this Union in a real fight!—**Gen. U.S. Grant**

Far as I can tell, the Confederates are losin' terribly. It's a mighty shame, too. Nashville's a Southern town to its core. I hate to see those young men, men I probably know, droppin' like flies down there. The field is stained red with their blood. Gen'ral Hood has pulled his men back two miles yonder. There doesn't seem to be much hope.—**Nashville housewife**

The Yankees started bombardin' us with artillery. We were no match for them. Men dyin' everywhere. I can't take it. The sound of guns and sufferin' is makin' me crazy!—**Confederate soldier**

As the sun rose on Nashville, I couldn't help but feel like we'd already lost the battle. Thomas' army started another attack, stronger than yesterday's. The whole Confederate army began retreatin', runnin' for safety wherever they could find it.—**Confederate soldier**

I thought I was home free when I heard the sound of horse hooves. The Yankees had sent their cavalry. They captured me and marched me back to Nashville.*—**Confederate soldier**

*About 4,000 Confederate soldiers were captured as prisoners in the Battle of Nashville. No one knows how many Confederates were killed.

I'm one of the lucky ones that got away. My guess is there's only 5,000 left of Hood's 40,000 man army. Hood himself resigned with shame. The Battle of Nashville was a disaster for the Confederates.—**Confederate soldier**

Way to go Gen. Thomas!

General Grant,
I followed your orders and traveled to Nashville only to find that the Confederates had been neatly cleaned out by Gen. Thomas. Seems he wasn't too slow after all.—**Gen. John A. Logan**

Union general Ulysses S. Grant at Appomattox Court House, Virginia...President Lincoln assassination by Southerner John Wilkes Booth...Vice President

woman in the world...2006...The Covenant becomes the first black book to reach number 1 on the New York Time's nonfiction paper back best seller list... 2007...Oprah Winfrey opens the Oprah Winfrey Leadership Academy for Girls in South

We are weak with few men and less supplies. Grant combined all remaining Union forces, including Sherman's army. I must muster as many men as I can find and lead this Confederacy in a brave stand against the Union.—**Gen. Lee**

Once again I take a position as general. This time, my men are exhausted and frail. I have what is left of the Army of Tennessee and volunteer soldiers from all over the South. We are 20,000 against Sherman's 60,000.—**Gen. Johnston**

We have left Petersburg and are marching as fast as we can to safety with the Union fresh on our heels. My men are moving slowly. They have had no food for nearly a week. My heart breaks for these poor, tired, brave soldiers.—**Gen. Lee**

The Confederacy has sent Johnston and a scraggly group of men to stall us from meeting Grant at Richmond. They pose no threat to us with their small numbers. Their ranks are now made mostly of generals and commanders after their fighting men have either died or deserted. They can hardly be called an army.—**Union soldier**

Gen. Forrest wouldn't give the order for us to stop fightin'. We were obviously outnumbered by the Union, but we kept on. He was relentless and defiant to the last. Finally, with much reluctance, Gen. Forrest ordered us to surrender. He agreed to return home and live peacefully. Then he turned to us and said, *"You have been good soldiers, you can be good citizens."* And that was it, my fightin' days were over.—**Confederate soldier**

We've no chance if we continue to wait here in siege. I've got 55,000 weak men while Grant has 120,000 strong men waiting to fight. If we can't win this war by strength, we'll have to find a way to outsmart those Yankees.—**Gen. Lee**

When we arrived at Appomattox, a small group of Yankees blocked our road. Gen. Lee ordered us to attack. I charged, tired and weak. Just as I drew my gun to shoot, I saw thousands of Union troops step up behind the men. I stopped in my tracks and slowly lowered my gun. The "small group of Yankees" was a huge army!—**Confederate soldier**

I have no choice now but to surrender, or lose everything.—**Gen. Lee**

He walks toward me slowly, with dignity. He is dressed in his finest Confederate uniform, clean, unblemished gray covered in polished, distinguished medals. His surrender is noble. He saved the lives of his few soldiers still living and turned the Confederate Army into the hands of the Union. Gen. Lee is a strong leader and a worthy opponent. He should hold his head high. Finally, this brutal war can come to an end.—**Gen. Ulysses S. Grant** on Robert E. Lee's surrender

I feel the sweat bead on my neck and forehead. My worst shame—surrender*—is a reality. Gen. Grant can do whatever he wants with me and my men. Shame us, put us to death…I fear the worst.—**Gen. Lee**

My terms of surrender are simple: lay your weapons down and return home peacefully. Generals and commanders can keep their swords and horses.—**Gen. Grant**

Lee surrenders at Appomattox Court House

*Although Lee surrendered on April 9, the official surrender did not take place until April 12, 1865.

Gen. Grant's most gracious offer is astounding! Not only does he spare our lives, he spares my dignity in letting me keep my dress sword and horse.—**Gen. Lee**

Men, distribute 25,000 army food rations to the Confederate troops right away and order the celebration of surrender to be stopped. The Rebels are our country-men again.—**Gen. Grant**

It was a somber walk through two long columns of Union soldiers as each of us slowly laid our weapons in a large pile. All of sudden, Gen. Chamberlain ordered the Union troops to salute us in a sign of respect. It was a moment I will never forget.—**Confederate soldier**

This is the end for me. Three years respected as a president, reduced to a prisoner in chains. The Union captured me here in Irwinville, Georgia, an unknown city that will now forever remember my shame. They're going to lock me up in Fortress Monroe in Virginia. I'll be tried for treason against the United States government. Part of me wonders, what have I done? So many men are dead. Homes destroyed. Cities burned and pillaged. Still, I'll forever be proud of my men and the way they fought for the great South.—**Jefferson Davis***

*Jefferson Davis was locked in a gunroom for only a few days, then released after a physician advised it would be good for his health. Davis was tried for treason in 1866; in 1867, he was released on bail. He traveled the world and returned to the United States as a civilian. He spent his time writing a book called *The Rise and Fall of the Confederate Government.* He died a free man in New Orleans at age 81.

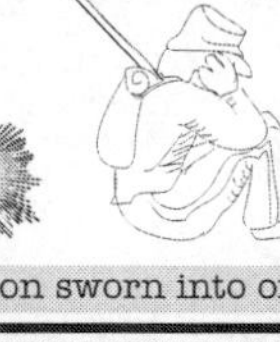

I have plans to restore the Union peacefully and quickly.—**Abraham Lincoln**

Andrew Johnson sworn into office…John Wilkes Booth shot and killed in Bowling Green, Virginia…President Johnson submits plan for Restoration of South

Africa… 2008… Barack Obama wins presidential election becoming first African American president-elect… 2009…Barack Obama is inaugurated as the first African American President …Michelle Obama is the first African American First Lady…

Reconstruction

Reconstruction: the recovery and rebuilding period following the Civil War

Can you believe the war is finally over? The weight of the world has been lifted from my husband's shoulders. I can see it in his eyes. And we are going to Ford's Theatre to see a play tonight! A night of lighthearted fun—I cannot wait!—**Mary Todd Lincoln**

POP! What was that? Part of the play? Women are shrieking! A man has leaped onto the stage, yelled, and run off. The president slumps in his chair! I see blood! Can it be true?! Did someone just shoot our president?!—**usher**, Ford's Theatre

Stop that man!—**Major Henry Rathbone**

Everyone is sobbing. Our president died early this morning. May God have mercy on this country.—**newspaper reporter**

I accept this office of President of the United States with a heavy heart.—Vice President **Andrew Johnson**

He was in that barn and wouldn't come out. So we set it on fire! I saw my chance, and took it. I shot him. I shot and killed that John Wilkes Booth.—**Union soldier***

*The manhunt for John Wilkes Booth was the largest in history, involving 10,000 federal troops, detectives, and police.

Here are the latest statistics, Sir: 618,000 soldiers dead; probably 100,000 civilians killed too, Sir. That includes the North and South, Sir. And we know that disease killed twice as many as those who died in battle.—**Union soldier** *

*The Civil War death toll is more than the total killed in battle in the American Revolution, War of 1812, Mexican War, Spanish-American War, World War I, World War II, Korean War, Vietnam, and Gulf War—all combined!

The Legend of *Taps*

In 1862, Union Army Captain Robert Ellicombe looked over the battle scene. He heard the groan of a wounded soldier. Although, he did not know if the soldier was a Union soldier or a Confederate soldier, the captain crawled through the battle amidst gunfire and carried the soldier to the medical tent. When he got back, he found that the soldier was a Confederate, but he was already dead. He recognized the face of the soldier and realized it was his own son. Because the son was a Rebel, he was not allowed to have a full military burial. Only one musician, a bugler, was allowed to play. The father asked the bugler to play a song that was found in the pocket of his son's uniform. The bugler played the song that became known as *Taps.*

This story is legend, not historically accurate

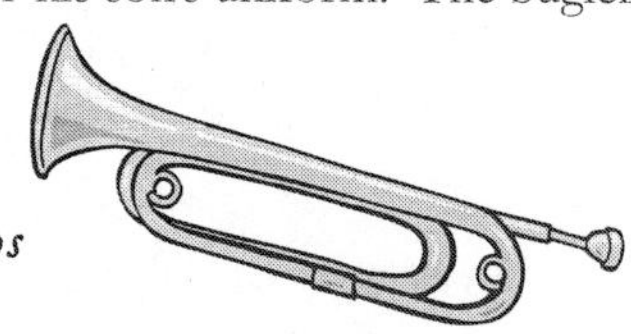

The True Story of *Taps*

General Daniel Butterfield was dissatisfied with the customary firing of three rifles at the end of military burials. He altered a French bugle call into what is now known as *Taps.* The song became very popular, and within months it was sounded by both the Union and Confederate armies.

This story is the true story of *Taps*. Not as fun and romantic as the Legend!

When we said our vows years ago, I was just a child. Jefferson was 18 years my elder. My momma almost cried when I said I wanted to marry him. But we've had a happy life together. Full of struggles, I suppose, but happy. I never thought I'd be the First Lady of the Confederacy, not in a million years! But I stand by Jefferson in everything. Right now he's locked up, accused of treason since the great South lost this Civil War. But I'm staying right here outside his jail cell. I'll fight for his release until I feel him back in my arms again, no matter how long it takes.—**Varina Howell Davis***

*Jefferson Davis was released in 1867 thanks to his wife's unrelenting requests for his freedom.

Everything is destroyed! Houses burned. Fields barren. Animals dead or dying—I can count their ribs. What has happened to our beautiful South?—**Confederate soldier**

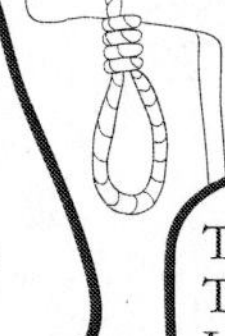

My lifeless body hangs on the scaffold. Three guilty men wave in the wind beside me. They accused me of conspiring to kill Abraham Lincoln. I did no such thing!—ghost of **Mary Surratt**

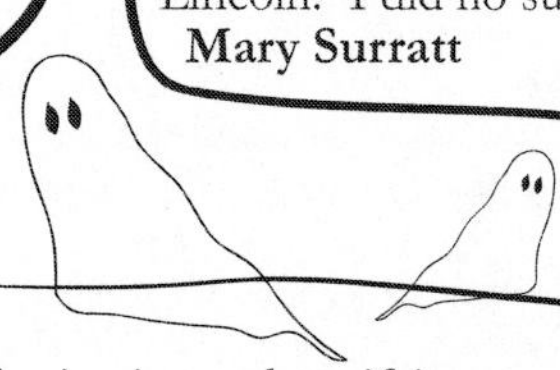

If these old walls could talk, they would tell a history so fascinating and terrifying, no student would ever tire of learning about American events. I was built years ago, before any of these men were even born. My walls were erected for protection, but just look at them now. Spirits seem to haunt this sad and forlorn place, and will forever more.—**Fort Monroe**

...All Confederate states except Mississippi readmitted to Union...Six Confederate officers form anti-black society, Ku Klux Klan...1866...Congress passes Civil

Susan Rice is the first African American woman to become the United States' U.N. Ambassador... Eric Holder is the first African American Attorney General of the United States... 50-year-old pop icon Michael Jackson dies of cardiac arres t...Venus

Did I ever think I would see this day? No, sir! No more slavery—thanks to the Thirteenth Amendment to the Constitution. What a day, what a day! Free at last! Praise the Lord!—**former slave**

We've got to keep these free blacks under control! We'll wear white robes and hoods and terrorize them at night—they'll think we're spirits of Confederate soldiers! That'll keep them in their place.—**Ku Klux Klan member***

* The Ku Klux Klan was a secret society organized by Southerners that used violence and terror to maintain "white supremacy."

I thought the war was over! But they passed that Military Reconstruction Act and Union troops are still here—occupying the South! It's like pouring salt into a fresh wound. And those Northerners wonder why we're bitter?!—**Southern schoolteacher**

Carpetbaggers! Scalawags! Just look at them taking advantage of our pain to make money for themselves! Why, if one of them comes into my shop, I'll shoo him out so fast his hat will spin right off his head!—**Southern shopkeeper**

Thank ya, suh for these clothes to wear and food for my fam'ly. We have nothin'. Don't know what we'd do without the Freedman's Bureau to help us. It seems like everyone else is ag'in us.—**freed slave***

*The Freedman's Bureau was a federal agency formed to help former slaves get food, clothing, medical care, and fair treatment after the war.

Tenants ain't got no chance. I don't know who gets the money, but it ain't the poor. It gets worse every year—the land gets more wore out, the price for tobacco gets lower, and everything you got to buy gets higher. Like I said, I'm trying to 'be content' like the Bible says and not to worry, but I don't see no hope.—**sharecropper's wife**

We have great hopes for the Fourteenth Amendment! It grants equality to all citizens, but big problems still exist between blacks and whites in the South. Southern states have passed Black Codes—laws to deny former slaves their rights. There is still such violence...will they ever embrace each other?—**Northern Congressman**

So far from engaging in a war to perpetuate slavery, I am rejoiced that slavery is abolished. I believe it will be greatly for the interest of the South. So fully am I satisfied of this that I would have cheerfully lost all that I have lost by the war and have suffered all that I have suffered to have this object obtained.—**Robert E. Lee***

*Robert E. Lee spent the rest of his life as President of Washington and Lee University in Lexington, Virginia

I cannot help but feel sad and depressed...at the downfall of a foe who fought so long and valiantly, and had suffered so much for a cause, though that cause was, I believe, one of the worst for which people ever fought.—**Ulysses S. Grant**

Today, I have been elected to the United States Senate! I'm the first black man elected to the U.S. Senate! I must work to protect the rights of my black brethren. They have a steep hill to climb.— **Hiram Revels**, Mississippi

I'll be the first black man to cast my vote after the Fifteenth Amendment grants blacks the right to vote. My parents were slaves...and here I am! What a privilege! What an honor! I can't wait to vote!—**Thomas Mundy Peterson**

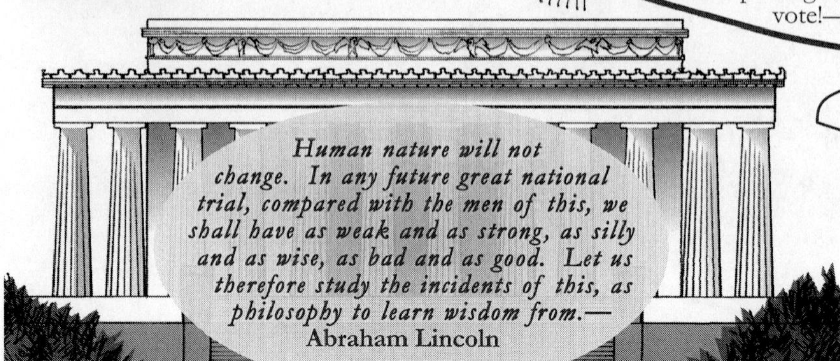

Human nature will not change. In any future great national trial, compared with the men of this, we shall have as weak and as strong, as silly and as wise, as bad and as good. Let us therefore study the incidents of this, as philosophy to learn wisdom from.—
Abraham Lincoln

Rights Act...1868...14th Amendment to the Constitution guarantees equal rights...1870...15th Amendment grants blacks right to vote.

and Serena Williams are the first African American world doubles tennis champions...Disney unveils The Princess and the Frog, the studio's first animated film featuring an African American princess.